CAROL D. MITCHELL

Employee's Only

cdmbooks@aol.com

CDMBOOKS@AOL.COM

Twitter: @suzy1493

A division of CDMBOOKS

Concord, California

This is a work of fiction. Names, characters, places and incidents either are the product of the author's imagination or are used fictitiously. Any resemblance to actual persons, living or dead, events, or locales is entirely coincidental.

All rights reserved
Copyright © 2019 by Carol D. Mitchell
Cover design by Gregg Banks
Printed in the United States of America
cdmbooks@aol.com

Carol Denise Mitchell

TABLE OF CONTENTS
EMPLOYEES ONLY

Chapter 01 — What is an Employee..............................Page 07

Chapter 02— Your Work Experience............................Page 12

Chapter 03— My Job Search.......................................Page 15

Chapter 04— Job Prep 101...Page 19

Chapter 05— Using Social Media...............................Page 24

Chapter 06— Interview Q&A......................................Page 29

Chapter 07— Employee Company Search................... ...Page 33

Chapter 08— Interview Rep.......................................Page 40

Chapter 09 —Organize Your Office.............................Page 49

Chapter 10— Your Rights, Temporary.........................Page 52

Chapter 11— Human Resources.................................Page 56

Chapter 12— The Employee Handbook.......................Page 60

Chapter 13— Sexual Harassment................................Page 70

Chapter 14 —Worker's Compensation.........................Page 72

Chapter 15— Letters/Samples....................................Page 79

Chapter 16 —Unemployment Insurance.......................Page 97

Chapter 17— Fired/Unemployment II..........................Page 98

Chapter 18— Worker's Comp., II................................Page 102

Chapter 19— EEOC..Page 109

Chapter 20— Job APS/Android..................................Page 124

The Introduction

My name is Carol Denise Mitchell. I am the writer of *Your Rights, What Employer's Do Not Want you to know*. It is a book that was generated to specifically help employees on a wide range of topics from how to find a job, to how to preserve your interest in a job. I never went to law school, but I have been in the workplace long enough to write a book that will be useful to those of you who enter the workforce after me. This time we're going to get ready to send you to work properly and give you more knowledge on the workplace as it may pertain to you. 2020 Job Trends are proof that though some things stay the same, the workplace is preparing now for Millennials. Pretty soon it will be out with the old guard and in with the new and employer's trending focus will be predicated more on Social and emotional intelligence in the work place. They're saying use the new year to refresh and look back on your career. And, if you don't like where you are; now is the time to change. Trends remain their primary focus on how companies will hire. While, baby boomers retire most of these decisions truly promote upward mobility as in education. Future work places will be focusing largely on millennials and these young folks will be leading teams and getting promotions to "C" level suites; but in my reflections, I have ascertained that most work paradigms will not change. Communication is going to be relatively important; but work rules, employment, unemployment, and work policies will be the same. 2020 Trends will find the focus: will be predicated on a healthier cultivation of advanced emotional intelligence at the high-levels to attract, and to keep high level skilled employees. We're going to see more automation that they're predicting will be revolutionary. If you're thinking Jetsons, those robotic concepts could happen for future trends in the workplace; but the old guard still wants Millennials to get an education. So, if you're thinking about perhaps getting a degree in Artificial Intelligence, know that future trends data regarding the workplace are projecting a sort of "co-bot" where they're saying such relationships. You're on the right track. This will be beneficial for those seeking automated kind of changes in the workplace. Terminology in scope: From LinkedIn Learning, Busuu and Coursera to Udemy, edX and The Khan Academy, many lessons and modules meet budget constraints and should be an ask of any employee who wants to exceed. The pros are also predicting that millennials will have a shorter attention span because whereas back in the day, a worker stayed on a job from 2-25 years, the average tenure now is 2.9 years as millennials are pruned to branch out in their own companies or are crafty contractors with short long-term attention spans. I have been a manager, a mother, a writer, a wife, and a friend. Today, I am here specifically to help you get the job you deserve and to help you keep it. Therefore, I must say as I did in my first book the following: The use of this guide is for readers who want easy access to personal and published information regarding employment rights. As more fully set forth in the terms of your using this guide, the data provided here is for general information purposes; it is not a determination of your legal rights nor your responsibilities under the law. I am not a lawyer, and none of the information contained in this guide is or should be defined as legal advice. I am not engaged in the practice of law, and no attorney-client relationship is being created. Any information communicated to any lawyer via this guide does not have any confidentiality protection of the attorney/client privilege. Laws do change often. This guide contains information that is current to date and the purpose of this guide is to provide you with information that will be illuminative in your job search. If you are seeking legal advice, find a qualified lawyer in your area. If you need help in finding a lawyer, call your local, county, state bar association, or check out the information below.

- National Employment Lawyers Association, (NELA) @ http://www.nela.org/home.cfmNELA is the largest and most effective plaintiff employment lawyer organization in the United States. The headquarters is in San Francisco, California.

- Workplace Fairness at Http://www.workplacefairness.org. This is an excellent web-site for _lay_ people to learn about their rights as employees and how to save or get their job back

Make sure your job complies with employment law

From day one on a new job, look for the colorful, ***"Required Posters for the Workplace."*** Search for the posters in the kitchen or the copy room. Familiarize yourself with the Occupational Safety and Health Administration (OSHA) laws, workers compensation, Equal Employment Opportunity Commission, EEOC and the Department of Fair Employment and Housing, DFEH laws. Learn who the company doctor is on the OSHA posters in case you get hurt on the job. Look for the treatment facilities address and telephone number.

How to find a job and keep it

Later, you will know what the definitive definitions of the employee are as they pertain to you and the company that wants your skills. Flower grow wherever you choose to work and let us get going. You're going to learn a lot. With this guide, you're going to enhance your overall work growth, while you find sample letters that will help you write well and be precise. You're going to have sample letters to reference if you need to address growth and or problems on the job. It's important to remember that you must always maintain your integrity on the job. Let's answer a big question. What is truly an employee?

End of Chapter Refresher

1. Be a good employee first; and the wisest employee later.

2. You must always maintain your integrity on the job and on your employment application

3. Know your role as an employee. Fulfill that role.

4. Know your employment rights.

5. First day on the job, familiarize yourself with posters.

Chapter 1

What Is an Employee

Now is the time to get a better understanding of what the true definition of employee is because the employer will confuse the issue, depending on legal reasons. Generally, the definition of the word, "employee" has varying meanings. When it comes to you knowing what role "employee" in a company is, it may be essential to your privileges if a company hires you to perform a distinct form of labor or work. Your offering to a specific job and or, the industry has a lot to do with what job you were hired to do, and how your skills, and or education and experience match, and can positively influence ongoing residual profits for the company. Work titles cover a wide range of professional business from accountants to lawyers. With the recent boom in technology, some professional work titles are transcending conventional definitions and are changing with trends. Some employees, *(depending on the work contract),* are permanent and they receive a guaranteed wage. Others may be hired as temporary employees, contract employees, or as consultants.

What the State Labor Code says about being a Temporary Employee:

It is most important to know what the State Labor Code, 201.5 says about being a Temporary Employee, because this is one of the biggest questions temporary employees in America have. "Temp" as we're called in America want to know if they have the same benefits as a "regular" employee in the workplace. In this New self-help guide, *"Employee's Only,"* the answer is astounding! So, that this help guide remains #1 in the industry of aiding employees, we resorted to the law as stated before care of Leginfo.ca.gov 201.3. For purposes of this book the following definitions do apply:

Temporary services definition

This means that an employing unit that contracts with clients or customers to supply workers to perform services for the client and or its customers that perform all the following. Keep in mind that "all" entails performing many of the duties of a "Regular" vested employee. This means you're entitled basically to the same protections of the "Regular" employee. Should issues ensue on the job, this means your options for resolution are like and in some cases equal to a "Regular" employee. So, if any of the following methods apply to your services, you're entitled to the same remedies as a 'Regular" employee.

You: Negotiate with clients and customers for matters such as the time and place where the services are to be provided, including the type of work, the working conditions, and the quality and prices of services. Self-employed employees who own entire businesses are usually in trade for themselves; however, if they have just a person working for them, they may be considered an employee of the client, (employer) for tax purposes.

Honesty is the best Policy

The purpose of this book is to give you the advantage in finding a job and keeping it. Your success begins with you. Your integrity is one of the most important things you must give to an employer. There are no shortcuts in being honest. Honesty is still the best policy, for there is no place in the industry from either side to lie. Never make anything up before or after the hiring process. Be honest. Be open to clarifying the mistakes you may have made in life, in the past. Justify events by keeping a daily calendar whether you're inclined to do so or not; because if you know that nobody expects you to be perfect, you will be able to preserve your integrity, truthfully. Even if nothing really happened that day on the job, you will be able to cite that as well, so long as you know of your innocence and the employer believes in second chances.

Write it Down

Maintaining notes on the job is essential and one of the most important aspects of writing it down is to jog your memory and record the facts. Your notes sustain important times and dates. It edifies your involvement. It proves through employment records your whereabouts as it pertains to events on the job. Always keep notes on the job, for they will keep notes on you!

It's your Future

When you read this guide take it seriously. Know that it was created with your best interest on the job in mind, which is why I aim to make the job finding processes as easy for you as possible. No one in the world will have the diamond in their hand to prosper like you do when you're prepared to deliver excellent performances in your new job. Implement these proven suggestions maturely, for I know they work. You will be on your way to not only finding a job, but you're going to be a solid winner in keeping your new job. You're going to know what to say, how to say it, and how to live up to all the promises you will make to your new employer. You're going to grow and show other's how to grow with you. You're going to be armed with ways to preserve your interest on and off the job. You're a winner so long as you take who you are serious. Getting and keeping a job will be a piece of cake. Cultivate the best parts of you. As a person looking for a job, remember that you're not alone. With *"Employee's Only,"* you have a friend that will stand as a reminder to you, that you have value. *Employees Only* know how to optimize what's out there for you. Once you're good, my advice is that you purchase another of these books for a friend. Wouldn't it be a great idea if success could be spread universally? This is the positive tool you have been waiting for. So, let's get started.

How to find a job

When things get tough and your search for a job becomes redundant, help is on the way. There are thousands of ways to look for employment. But how many of these methods are productive for you? Let's try to help you optimize your job search, in lessened times. Okay, so high school is over. Mom and dad want you to get a job and there are a few things you're not all that sure about, like where do I look first? The summer was great. You enjoyed the fun in the sun and now you're ready to get your feet wet in a new job search. The first thing you're going to need to do is to believe in yourself well enough to build a solid job resume.

Chapter 2

Your Work Experience

Next, sit down in a very comfortable place. Get to know who you really are when it comes to your job experience. Think back to when you worked at the print shop with mom or dad or, when you were a volunteer at camp. Did you sell *Girl Scout* cookies? Did you organize that "Cake sale" event outside of the supermarket? How well did you do in sales? Yes. You have important job experience, you can't overlook. This will be important to your skillset, especially after you graduate from high school. You may feel you lack job experience. Help is on the way. Many applicants don't total all their real-life work experience! So, all the way up to when you graduated from high school or college, please calculate your true work experience, even count what you did in that "Cake sale." Don't cheat yourself, because maybe you did not get pay for work. Learn how to adequately itemize your work life experiences by using your skills dating back to when you were a kid, when you first began working or babysitting for others. Many individuals who set out to look for work these days don't know how to do this simple task. Let me show you how. TIP: If you had a fundraiser for two-years as a child and, you created drinks, snacks and such for a church or yard sale, write that experience down. You're not even 10 and already you have these proven skills:

1. Two-years of sale's experience, (church bake sale)

2. Created posters (for dad's printing shop)

3. Two-years of cash register experience

4. Conducted/ organized prayer group for charity for two-years

5. Baked and sold cakes for a church "Cake sale"

6. Earned over $500.00 for charity.

<u>Example #1</u>. Your father owned a printing shop. You helped make sales to customers, and stocked shelves. Or, you were once a Girl's Scout. You led in cookies sales. You created the posters for an event and talked to potential customers. At the end of the day, you sold out because your customer service skills are awesome!

<u>Example #2</u>. You may not have been paid for this job, but you do have the on the job experience. Now, it's time for you to get credit for work experience you may have otherwise overlooked. Don't forget to add your customer service skills. Use dad and other witnesses who saw you perform such duties as references. In fact, if you worked with your father/mother for many years selling printing services to customers, here are the skills you have acquired:

Carol Denise Mitchell

Your special skills

1. Customer service skills

2. Stocked shelves, organized

3. Sales experience/copier services

4. Cash register experience

5. Store management skills

6. Extra Duties: Open/closed business and set the alarm system.

In order to fully optimize this experience in totality, add all your work experience within the scope of your overall training dating back to when you first began working. Why? Because many workers out of college believe they don't have enough work experience to apply for a certain job. You must use all the experience, whether you were paid for such duties or not. To further verify this experience to a potential employer, ask your parents, uncles or aunts who witnessed such activities to certify this experience for you via a written declaration or through photographs and sworn statements. Add this important customer service and sales experience to your resume and you're on your way for that incredible first job experience.

Chapter 3

My Job Search

One thing everybody knows about looking for a job is how boring it can get, sometimes. Job searching is not the ideal way for most people to spend their valuable day. I am sure you can think of a million more things you'd rather be doing than looking for a job. But you can turn this task into something positive, so be on your mark. When you're looking for a job be serious. Always keep in mind that you are indeed the best employee for any job. Job hunt with the same tenacity and commitment as if you're looking for a vacation spot or a date. Please learn to enjoy it until you get the job that you deserve. There are so many places you can venture into to find work if you remember this important truth. *"You are the best person for the job!"* First, we must figure out what job you're looking for and go after it. If you're interested in being a secretary, don't just focus on *Monster*, or *Indeed* or job postings that a million other people are looking at, climb out of the box. Be on your mark. Be ready to get to the finish line sooner than later. Treat this job employment search as something special, because you are special. You are the best person for the job! No matter how tired you may get of looking for employment, remain positive, no matter how long it takes, remain firm in your resolve to find and be the best person on the job. Why? Because you are the person your next job is looking for. No one is going to be able to shine like you are.

Resources: Facebook, Twitter, YouTube

Even the President of the United States knows the values of Social Media, so why shouldn't you? Facebook, Twitter, YouTube and more are fabulous ways to think out of the box in your new job search! The more people who know you're looking for work, the better chance you have of connecting for work. Watch your job finding resources grow! Have fun. Seek employment and get likes on Facebook and Twitter. Ask your friends about work opportunities. Tell them you're looking for work as a secretary. I want to know if you have any leads? "Do you know anyone in our Facebook group who is hiring?" Make sure you're ready with a nice crisp resume, to present to whoever is ready to receive it. In fact, have at least 3 versions of your resume for your job search. Spend one day crafting and designing a resume. *"Do not use a photo in your resume."* No matter how cool it becomes don't do it. The element of surprise is going to get you this job. Keep reading to find some neat ways to get out of the future employer's junk piles. Be on your way to be the person that is chosen for the job. Read on!

End of Chapter Refresher

1. As a temporary worker, keep in mind that "all" entails performing many of the duties of a "Regular" vested employee. This means you're entitled basically to the same protections of the "Regular" employee.

2. Do not lie on your employment application.

3. Learn how to write down job skills dating back to the lemonade stand, church cake sales, and print shop.

4. Make at least 3-different resumes

5. Remember, you're the best person for the job!

Cool Places to look for work

Network at Career Centers

We hear you! You're looking for a job! I got you. Here is a great place to get started, The Career Center. Back in the day when I was looking for a job in Property Management, I found career centers throughout California to be a great place to commence my job search. There, I met lifelong friends at the career centers in Concord, California. Often, we traded information that was helpful to us all, including how to create Yahoo and Gmail accounts. The first thing to do is Google career center locations. Search for the closet centers to your residence. Next, sign up with at least two of them closest to your home. This is a great resource for those who aim to take the job search seriously, in a comfortable setting where you're not interrupted by family or friends. The career center is usually a division of your state's Human Resources and Unemployment division, and you don't have to pay to use the in-house resources, computers or facility. Being in this environment gets you out of the house for a few hours and on your way to applying for many work opportunities, with fewer interruptions. Here are four special employment agencies that have been around long enough to provide you with a leg up on the competition. Begin your job search here for their longevity in the business. When you go to apply at an agency, be prepared to take a Microsoft Word test, a typing test and sometimes a personality assessment test. There are dozens of agencies to work for, so narrow it down to the best. Here are four of my favorite Temporary agencies. Remember this about temporary agencies. Develop a great relationship with them. And, you could land a full-time job!

FOUR GREAT AGENCIES

- **Kelly Services -(248) 362-4444**

This is a great company that has been around a long time. They began in 1946 and are an industry leader. They have employed over one million workers. Be prepared to take and ace the assessment test.

- **Randstad - (770) 937-7000**

This is a great company that has been around since 1960. They have locations in 39 countries. They too will assess computer skills.

- **Adecco - (602) 266-6930**

Is another great company. They have been around for 50 years and they are a member of the National Minority Supplier Development Council. They also perform computer testing.

- **Robert Half - (650) 234-6000**

Was founded in 1948. Robert Half was added to Fortune Magazine World's Most Admired Companies Lists several times and has over 400 locations throughout the world. Testing is required!

Chapter 4

Job Prep 101

You know the definition of employee. You have calculated your work experience(s). You have 3 great resumes representing the totality of your work experience. Prior to going to the center, set aside 3-hours a day for your job search. Do not let anything get in the way of your job search goals. Here is how the Career Centers work. They're going to register you. They will have you sign in every day. They do this in order to maintain funding for the facility through the Employment Development Department. Next, you're going to have access to computers, printers, and job postings that are difficult to find at home or on your home computer. There are multiple advantages to being able to search for a job inside the comfortable confines and setting of a Career Center. The great thing about Career Centers is that once you get there you can set up an email address specifically geared towards your job search. Next, you can store your 3 resumes in your new Yahoo/Gmail/AOL account for easy access.

<u>What's in your job portfolio?</u>

Here is what you're going to be sending out during your job search: 3 great resumes, one job cover letter, all your job references and an itemized list of all of your job experience. Remember; limit your resume to one page. Prepare your resume in *Times New Roman 10* font. Your cover letter should be one-page *Times New Roman 12 font*. Make sure your references are willing to be there for you for at least one year. Continually update your references when a potential employer may be giving them a call.

Career Center Tips

In your leisure time, you can read the postings on the board and apply for jobs that suit your proven skills. Take your time to utilize this facility to optimize your job search and relax. Remember, that while you're conducting this search, do not leave out the opportunity to search for state, or government jobs that may require a test. In fact, began writing another list for state and government state test. Go to your state's website. Find out what test are needed for the job and go to your local library for books that will help you prepare for a state or government job test. Because some job postings may be dated, if you're really interested in a career opportunity, write a letter to government and state offices to acquire more accurate/updated information on when a job will be opening and how, and/or when can you test for that position. Ask what test will be required to apply for a city, state or government job. Create a calendar. Book your test appointment dates and study for it at the local library.

If you test for a state or government job and score well, you will get calls from dozens of offices! Hit the books. TIP: Government, state jobs have free study guides at the public library. Take a friend with you for a companion to help you prepare for the test!

Avoid burn out

If you're effective at your job search, it won't be necessary to go to the Career Center every day until you find a job. Once your resume and materials are well-prepared, you merely need to make time to apply for jobs. When you go to the Career Center, go at least 3 times a week so you don't get burned out during your job search. Stay positive, stay fresh. Stay determined to find a job. Treat going to the Career Center the same way you'd treat going to work. Don't waste your time, be productive. When you're at the Career Center go there for the sole purpose to find a job.

Be Helpful

You're going to find that there are people at the Career Center, who may need your help. You're probably great at setting up a Yahoo or Gmail account or you can show someone new how to click on "New" in Microsoft word to create a generic resume/letter. Someone else may be struggling. Spend a few minutes to help another. See how good it makes you feel. Helping others gives you a psychological boost. It can be most motivating during your own job search.

Talk to the counselors

Counselors at the job Career Centers are available to assist you in your job search and let you know when companies will be coming in to hire job seekers. Ask for the signup sheet to preserve your place at one of these most useful job fairs/seminars. They will be able to sign you up for seminars and for job fairs that aren't posted on the Internet. Counselors are a great resource for jobs that are not posted outside of the agency. When you approach one of these professionals at the center, make sure you let them know what kind of job you're looking for. They may have a resource for you, on the spot.

Ten Copies Only - Follow the Rules

The career center serves a lot of people. It's important to follow the rules, so everyone has a fair chance to get a job. Make sure that you don't exceed the limits of the posted rules regarding making copies and, the use of the fax machines. While you're at the career centers you're also in training for how you're going to comport yourself within your new work environment. Use it as a training ground for your new job. Because state and government offices are generally on a stringent budget, follow the rules. Ten copies mean just that, because many job seekers truly need these services, as well.

Don't forget to sign-out!

On any given day when you're done applying for jobs, there are some things you may forget. Once you sign off the computer for the day, clean up the place. Make sure you have signed out of your Yahoo and or Gmail accounts to protect your privacy. Keep it neat. Again, don't forget to sign out of your Yahoo/Gmail accounts and uncheck the box where it asks if you want to keep the password. Next, return the computer station back to the clean condition it was in when you arrived. The next day, begin by checking your email to ascertain if anyone responded to your resume. If you get a lead, respond within 24-hours. Good luck. Have fun finding your new job at the community career center!

<u>End of Chapter Refresher</u>:

1. Be serious about your job search

2. Be resourceful about your options

3. Be helpful to those in need

4. Be prepared to work full-time

5. Sign up for job fairs/seminars

<u>FOUR MORE GREAT AGENCIES</u>

1. Aerotek – Corporate 410-694-5100

2. Ultimate Staffing Services – 714-939-8600

3. Terra Staffing Group – 623-321-5151

4. Royal Personnel Services – 480-744-1279

Chapter 5

Using Social Media

So, you're at home and dinner is over. Mom and Dad are at the movies. You read *"Employee's Only,"* you're proud for posting many resumes at the job career center today. You're feeling good because your job portfolio is in place. You even helped someone get a Yahoo email account today. You have a date later, but you have some time on your hands. I have something for you to do. You are still looking for a job and things are looking good, but they can get better. It's Friday night. Your date won't be there for 3-hours, here's a great time to use your home computer to look for jobs in places where nobody else will be! That's right. A friend of yours got a job at Microsoft. You thought that was cool! You have the right skills. Like your friend, if you could only get an interview with someone in upper management, you know that once they see your resume, you can get the job. In fact, you will be able to do a great job and be an asset to the company. As I said earlier, the President of the United States has made tweeting quite popular. All the new Democrat presidential candidates are using Twitter too. Executives no longer are inaccessible to the average, every day person. Did you know that like it is for the President, Twitter is a great tool to get the message out? In fact, few job seekers think about non-conventional ways to look for jobs. Using Twitter is a new job search trend! Sometimes going to the career center and looking on *Monster* or *Indeed* gets boring and you're going to have to invigorate your job search and step up your game. You're one of millions of job searchers. You've been looking for a job for weeks and have gotten some replies, but not the gold.

Twitter Job Search Tips

Find out through Wikipedia, who owns that corporation that you want to work for and acquire their twitter address. Next, read all you can about this company. In rare instances you'll get the real name of valuable job resources. The information will be listed on the right side of the page for Microsoft that will tell you who the management contacts are. Copy that person's name as such. John Doe Microsoft, when that manager's name comes up @john doe on Twitter, attach your resume to a tweet. Next, attach a cover letter as such. If you're ambitious, here is how you can post using more than the thirty or so characters Twitter allows you to use. Go to PowerPoint. Create a beautiful job query letter on a one-page board, save as a PNG. Spell check your letter, see it as a billboard. Feel free to use this one! Post it with your tweet!

- According to Susan P. Joyce recruiters and employers do search Google for job candidates and I am hearing Google does love Twitter. Go ahead and leverage search engines optimizations (SEO) techniques in Twitter to make it easy for them to find you. I'm hearing do it not for just Twitter but also in Google and other searches. Thanks Susan P. Joyce!

Carol Denise Mitchell

Your Sample Query Letter

Dear BMC: June 8, 20_____

I am applying for the position of *Office Manager*, which was advertised recently on Craigslist. The position fits very well with my education, experience, and career interests.

According to the advertisement, your position requires excellent communication skills, computer literacy, and a specific degree in business. I do have the ability to initiate and work multiple priority projects concurrently. As you can see in my resume, my studies have included courses in marketing, business administration, business English, business communication(s), management information systems, and computer science. My on the job experience includes solid computer skills, front and back office management, and the ability to work well with others. I understand the position also requires a candidate who is team-oriented and can deal with business vendors both in and out of a pressure's environment.

They are all skills I developed both in my course work and in my long work history. I am looking forward to the opportunity of this interview and in working for a dynamic, internationally recognized company like yours. Therefore, I am confident that I can excel in the new position that you have available and begin work at your soonest convenience.

If you could schedule an interview with me, please call 925-435-XXXX. I will be available at your convenience.

Thank you for your consideration,

Sincerely,

John Doe

Enclosure: Resume

Twitter Query:

Dear John Doe, I have always wanted to work for Microsoft, I feel grateful I was able to find your twitter feed. My friend began working for you recently and loves his new job in Human Resources. Here is my letter! Guess what? No longer are you in a field of thousands of job seekers, your chances of getting that interview are better than they were before. Good luck. Enjoy your date tonight, you're about to get hired.

How to properly prepare for an interview

Your date was hot! To top it off, the next morning that manager from Microsoft saw your unique posting on Twitter. They liked it because he is really looking for someone like you who thinks out of the box. He loved your query letter and how you have been using the computer since you were five. In fact, he shot you back a contact to send your resume to. You did that and a few days letter, Microsoft called you in for an interview!

Until you get the job, do not end your career center contacts just yet, we have to get you prepared for your interview. The manager said he'd like to meet with you in downtown Oakland, California in 3 days. Guess what? There is some work to do. I am going to show you how. Your unconventional method of looking for a job has worked. Your resumes were on hand. You complied with Microsoft's request and sent them your best resume and they loved it. A few days later you have an interview. You have researched the company well. You're excited to let the company see how ready you are to work for them.

The job interview is the future employer's first impression of you. You must know the company and shoot your best shot. You must research the company fully. It's worth repeating! Give the best interview that you possibly can. Even though Microsoft surely is a worldwide company, use your skills to find out who manages Microsoft. Know the products they sell what's new, what's old. Generally, we know the products they sell, but there's always more to know. There is too a lot of work to do for interview day.

MORE INTERVIEW TIPS

1. Get plenty of rest the night before your interview
2. Be early, find nearby coffee shop relax, review materials
3. Be confident, friendly and respectful
4. Know in advance you'll get this job
5. Believe it and retrieve it
6. Smile, always and be very polite
7. Limit tough, trick answers with yes or no.

Chapter 6

Interview QA

Interview Questions/Answers

Interview Questions/Answers - What to expect - how to answer the questions. Here is hoping this sample interview Q & A will be helpful to preparing you for your upcoming interview. Good luck!

Interview Question: "Tell me a little about yourself, Carol."

Answer:

"My name is Carol. I graduated from *The Institute of Property Management*, with a Pass Superior. I love helping others and am seeking employment in a company like yours in order to facilitate my learned skills in this field of property management employment."

Interview Question: "Where did you learn about the position?"

Answer:

"The school I attended in Hayward, California had your company posted on the job board. I checked you out on Wikipedia. I knew your company would be the right place to work for my future employment goals."

Interview Question: "Tell me what you know about this company."

Answer:

"I know that you're a multi-national company, with headquarters in Oakland, California and you were founded by Sally Desmond in 1942. You were voted one of the top 5 companies to work for by Forbes Fortune 100 and your revenue rose from 50 to 100 billion, since the inception of your company."

Interview Question: "Why do you want the job?"

Answer:

"Considering your job growth, to me this has unique value for my job goals. I am seeking employment inside of a company like yours with proven growth and opportunities. Additionally, should I get this job, I'd use public transportation. This gives me time to explore the city more before assuming job duties."

Interview Question: "How did you prepare for the interview?"

Answer:

First, I read your job posting. I looked you up on the Internet. I visited and liked your *Facebook, LinkedIn* and other social media locations. I was so impressed with your company. I loved your mission statement, how each employee is a family member. I also prepared for this interview by getting plenty of rest to be prepared as best I could for the interview."

Interview Question: "Give me 3 reasons why we should hire you."

Answer:

1. "I am qualified for the job
2. I am dependable
3. I am seeking a long-term position, like this one."

Interview Question: "What are your greatest strengths?"

Answer:

"My greatest strengths are dependability; job readiness and I am a great team player. I understand that no one person truly has all the answers, but I am pliable. I am willing to share and learn in the context of employment. I know how to resolve conflict on the job and know that coupled with my learned experience, I would be the perfect person for this job."

Interview Question: "What are your weaknesses?"

Continued next page...

Answer:

"Considering that no one person is infallible, my weakness is also one of my strengths. I love working long hours. Someone may have to remind me that the work day is over. I am seeking employment to fall in love with. So, giving up and beyond of myself would be my weakness."

Interview Question: "How dependable are you?"

Answer:

"I am the most dependable person you'll ever know. The way I stay this way is by getting to the job at least one-half hour before I am due. This way, if there are traffic problems, it gives me ample time to adjust in getting to work on time if the car breaks down or something. My co-workers can also depend on my willingness to share learned-experiences for the enhancement of the team, and not only to bolster my knowledge."

Interview Question: "Have you ever been fired and why?"

Answer:

"I have never been fired. I am human and am not perfect. But I have been fortunate enough to meet former expectations on the job enough so that I have never been fired."

Interview Question: "How long do you see yourself with the company?"

Answer:

"As I stated from inception, I applied with this company because of your material growth in this business. Also, this job is within 10 minutes of my home. Should I get hired, I plan on working here until retirement. My job search was thorough in the sense I was looking for a company just like yours to grow in. I'd be related to have that opportunity."

Interview Question: "Are you willing to work overtime?"

Answer:

"Yes."

Interview Question: "If hired, when will you be available for the job?"

Answer:

"At your convenience!"

The secret to answering interview questions is to answer the question. Don't incorporate too much into the question. Be precise. Do your homework on the company. Read over the questions and answers as often as you can to be prepared for the interview! You will do just fine. Turn the negative, "Trick" questions, i.e., what are your weaknesses into one of your strengths.

End of Chapter Refresher

1. Looking for a job means thinking out of the box

2. Turn negative into positive

3. Career centers across the country are waiting for you

4. Preparation is key

5. Remember to shine at your job interview

6. Get plenty of rest the night before

7. Use Wikipedia to find out more about the company you're seeking to work for.

Chapter 7

Employee/Company Search

Research the Company

The job you applied for is in IT Management so, go to *Indeed* or *Monster* to view all postings Microsoft listed for this position. Study them. After finding out what is the job description for IT Management, as it pertains to Microsoft word, perform due diligence in your research. YouTube is a great place to research possible methodologies used in the IT Management field. It's also a great time to go to the public library to research Microsoft. Learn about what extra benefits they may be willing to give to employees. Here is a list of benefits most employees are seeking in today's fast paced work environment: When you're looking for a job, know what you want. Trending: Here are some of the most important features for today's employees. If you're looking for a long-term job, ask for all or some of the following benefits!

1. Health Insurance, COBRA and afterwork benefits

2. 401K Plan and Mutual Funds – Company's contributions

3. Worker's Compensation – (Hurt on the job)

4. Disability short and long term/State Benefits

5. Vacation, sick days and holidays

6. Leave of absence – Family Leave

7. Dental, Medical and Vision Care insurance

8. Job training – Upward mobility

9. Tuition, reimbursement opportunities

If you buy a book from *Barnes and Noble* or another bricks and mortar site, don't ruffle the pages too much. Keep the receipt so you can take the book back after your studies, if that's the case.

1. Check Dunn & Bradstreet

2. Check the Better Business Bureau/Complaints

3. Check Verify - to ascertain if the company might be defaulting on loans, and investors

4. Check YouTube - to see if employees are complaining on line about undesirable employment practices.

Watch YouTube Videos

Use all your resources to get the right answers and write them down. Once you have ascertained exactly what the IT Manager does within the frame of Microsoft, spend at least 3-hours reading everything. Research the duties back and forth. Memorize trending definitions and exceed the scopes of these in your interview. Don't lie. Be informed. Remember, how *"Employee's Only,"* taught you to use all your skills from sales, to team leadership in the Boys Scouts. All your experience is relative! Once you have studied what the job duties are, go back, brush up your resume to reflect real-life work experiences. Upon meeting the interviewer, you want to have at least 5-copies of your resume in a beautiful brown or black attaché case.

Let's Talk Resumes

There is something about you that Microsoft likes, and you have 3 resumes that don't reflect IT Management, excellence. It's time to create a tailor-made resume that better reflects your experience for the job. Let them know you know more than you could itemize on your resume. Immediately, you are an asset to them. Don't change the resume too much; rather, be able to expand on your work experience. From the beginning they see that you know how to think out the box. Use all resources to get the job. Name drop your friend, who was hired by the same company, the week before. Remember, if the manager really likes you, there could be 2-3 interviews to follow. You want to be prepared to accommodate any requests this manager may have for you. Edit your resume, perfectly and spell check it at least 3-times. You've already learned the company from A-Z. You graduated with great knowledge of IT Management. Now, after your research you undoubtedly want to meet the expectations that Microsoft has laid out in the job post. Call a friend. Run the job description over with them. Conduct a mock interview. Be objective. Be ready to take criticism if there are suggestions from that friend that will help you nail this upcoming interview. Now, that your research is done, and your resumes are looking good you must go to Office Depot. Get your attaché case.

You're confident, you are ready to go out there and get that job! Here is a sample of a resume. I have split up the job resume so you will see how to prepare it in ways that will highlight your optimum work experience. Remember to go beyond one-liners to tell the future employer, exactly what you did in your previous employment. Your *Career Objective* should explain what you're seeking in a job, and how what you're looking for correlates with your work experience and or education. On the following pages, you're going to view how to list work experience in ways that tells the employer how you functioned in similar work settings. Whether you're an entry level employee, up to manager, be precise in detailing former work experience, as to not leave ambiguity concerning your skills.

Important Resume Tips

1. Try to keep it on one page

2. Be sure to expand on work experience in details

3. Career Objective explains wants and abilities, briefly

4. Spell check, grammar check

5. All jobs should correlate beginning/end dates

Your Sample Resume (Explained)

CAREER OBJECTIVE

"Write a clear, well thought out career objective"

<u>Sample:</u> My *"Career Objective"* is to obtain an *Administrative Assistant* position comprising over ten-years of administrative and writing services. I worked for 3 executive-level professionals. I am seeking a position to incorporate education, proven administrative skills, and the uses of *Microsoft Word, Publisher* and *Excel, with capabilities* of fulfilling a diverse range of work obligations, as well. I am too seeking to coordinate and handle high volume projects fast and efficiently, while functioning in multiple roles as is needed in my *Administrative Assistant* role.

SKILLS

- MAC/Microsoft
- Word, Excel, PPT
- Superb Organization
- Supervisory Skills
- AMSI/Yardi/Excel
- Time Management Skills
- Database Management/IT
- Team Player/Mentor/Manager
- Internet Research/Media
- Outlook/Mozilla/PC's & MAC

IN WRITING DOWN JOB EXPERIENCE, GIVE DETAILS.
SENIOR IT MANAGER - 2010-2019 (Details)

CDM3Publishing.com - San Francisco, CA

Sample: Created core *Human Resources* materials. Lead IT management, including in the creation of a *new standard operating procedural guide.* Managed publishing, marketing, and the distribution of a manifold of published guides. Developed IT deployments, Q&A. Created all COBOL data filings. Posted to shared office site(s) bi-weekly. Used Outlook to generate travel arrangements/meetings. Also used advance skills in: *Word, Excel, Publisher* and *PowerPoint.* Hired/fired vendors and successfully managed a team of 5 IT management personnel.

IT MANAGER- 2005 – 2010 (Details)

Randstad Staffing Agency, San Ramon, CA

Lead, as IT Manager for 5 years at Berkeley Lab's *"Center for Functional Imaging."* Supported 5 corporate level officials in IT at AT&T, LBNL, and at a multi-unit off-site property. Communicated project status bi-weekly via regular emails to corporate staff. Organized time-sensitive deployments, front desk operations and copier room maintenance. Performed afternoon reception duties; and, created and organized electronic data. Maintained monthly work calendars, coordinated meetings, greeted visitors and wrote, proofed, mailed, and faxed correspondence, while performing other administrative duties per request of the department's need.

List your education for employment at the end of your resume.

EDUCATION

Mount San Antonio College, *Walnut, CA*

Institute of Internet Services, *Hayward, CA*

Internet Services Certification Completion - *2000*

MEMBERSHIPS & CHARITABLE ORGANIZATIONS

Volunteer Secretary: Chris Bush Relief Foundation, Union City, CA

<u>End of Chapter Refresher/Reminder!</u>

1. The Career Objective – explain
2. Start date, end dates, name of company
3. Detail work, duties, responsibilities
4. Keep resume to one page

Chapter 8

Interview Prep A-Z

Your resume got your foot in the door! Congratulations. Now, here is how you must show up for your interview. It's your last chance to prove to the potential employer that you are ready to come home to their work environment. Dress well. Don't wear wild, flashy colors unless you're told to specifically, by the employer. Keep hair out of eyes. Bath. Be fresh. Wear professional, well defined clothing, until you know exactly what the feel of the office is going to be. Here are some great examples of how you should look at your job interview.

How to dress for a job interview

You're ready to be hired! Your resumes are error free, classy and professional. When you're looking for a job remember to set one or two great outfits aside for your interview. It's as important as your resumes are. Invest in a good dark blue or black outfit for your job search. Guys wear new socks or a pair that is free of holes and free-fall threads. It's better to wear dark socks and dark shoes. Research high-end sales outlets for sale items like *Nordstrom* or *Macys* for finer clothing that is sold cheap, so you stand out in this interview:

Men: Matching dark blazer, dark pants that end at top of shoes. No flooding or highwater today. Wear a crisp white or off-white shirt open collar or thin tie. Make sure shoes are polished low heels. Hair should be well-groomed the night before off or above the eyes. Unless the employer specifically asked you to wear a wild color, like yellow or red "don't." Take this interview as seriously as you did the job search. Invest in a brown or black lightweight attaché case that makes you look great and shine. Inside of this case, make sure you have 10 copies of your resume, with another 10 copies of your cover letter, and at least 5 reliable job references, in case you're hired on the spot.

Women: Black or navy-blue dress a tad below the knee. Low to medium heels, black or dark blue. A pantsuit of the same dark color will work as well. Long hair should be coiffed out of the eyes, or over the shoulders so the employer will be able to give you direct eye contact, without competing with your hair. Don't wear large earrings. Wear small studs or diamond earrings that are barely there. "It's an interview; not a fashion show." Invest in a dark lightweight attaché case that makes you look great and shine. Inside of this case, make sure you have 10 copies of your resume, and 10 copies of your cover letter, and at least 5 reliable job references, in case you're hired on the spot.

The Mock Interview that worked!

Mock Interview Carol (Employer) & Michelle (Prospective Employee). This is the right way to interview for a job! Michelle is on time for a job as a Receptionist for *Company A*. *Company A* is seeking an employee who can operate a 24-line phone system fitted with voicemail. They need someone who thinks fast on her/his feet. Her/his job will receive and open/distribute mail. She/he are to answer all incoming calls, route such calls using the company directory via a specialized phone system. After lunch, her relief will take over the phones, while she/he delivers the inner office mail. Here is Michelle's interview that takes place on the ground floor of *Company A's* Conference room. Note how well-prepared Michelle is to get the job. Notice her great answers!

Carol: "Good morning, Michelle! I am Carol Mitchell. I am told you were here very early for your interview?" Carol asked, smiling. Michelle lives twenty-miles away. She asked her husband to drop her off one hour before her interview, so she'd be fresh for the job. Today, Michelle is dressed smartly in a dark pantsuit. Her shoulder-length hair is freshly coifed into a stylish bob, Michelle is ready in black, shining patent leather shoes. Michelle is also prepared with a black, snakeskin attaché case, that she bought on sale at *Staples* the day before. Upon introducing herself to the receptionist, a manager was called to interview Michelle for the Receptionist position. As soon as the interviewer, Carol Mitchell entered the lobby, Michelle stood up gracefully to greet her.

"You must be Michelle," Carol stated. Michelle smiled and greeted Carol back.

"I am so pleased to meet you. Would you prefer to be called Mrs. Mitchell or Carol?" Michelle asked her, correctly.

"Carol is fine, Michelle," Carol answered with a smile. Next, the two ladies walked to the conference room where coffee and refreshments awaited Michelle. Tip: (*Not a good time to eat doughnuts*). Focus!

"So, tell me Michelle, why do you want to work for *Company A?*" Carol asked. Michelle placed her black attache case on the table in front of her and crossed her hands until Carol asked her to please be seated. Tip: *(Be polite)*.

"Thanks for asking this question. I have researched *Company A*. I clearly value what this company stands for. You are number 2 in the country in sales and when the company grows, I read how for twenty-years this company is willing to invest in an employee's education toward upward mobility," Michelle answered. Carol smiled. It's great to hear when a potential employee wants a long-term career with the company. Tip: *(Limit answer responses)*.

"I have interviewed several others for this job, Michelle," Carol stated. "I am impressed that you took the time to acquaint yourself with the history of *Company A*," Carol said smiling. She continued.

"Michelle, how well can you manage busy phone lines?"

"Quite well," answered Michelle. She continued, "I love answering phones. On my last job I was employee of the month on a similar job. I answered multi-phone lines and, even got to know some callers. This afforded me the ability to route calls correctly, and swiftly, while I got to know those who worked within the company. I am comfortable, the busier the front desk becomes," Michelle answered, with a smile. After writing Michelle's answer's down, Carol asked more questions and indicated how pleased she was with

Michelle's answers by smiling. *Tip: (never offer more than what's asked of you in an interview that's going well).*

"May I see your resume, Michelle?" Carol asked. Michelle then opens her beautiful attache case to Carol's smile, because Carol is very impressed with Michelle's organized files. Michelle reaches inside, next she pulls out a fresh copy of her resume and, then hands it to Carol with a smile. Later, Carol examines it and continues to smile, while she reads the resume.

"I see you were at your last job for five-years?" Carol asked Michelle, as she looked up from the resume.

"Yes, ma'am. I was there six-years if you include the one year I worked as a temporary worker, through *Office Team*. I was very sad when the company left California after 100-years in business for Chicago. Had it not been for my mother's senior needs, I would have relocated to Chicago, to continue my work with the company. My mother has done a lot to cultivate my career. I wanted to take care of her in her senior years. So, I made a choice to stay in California. I treasure this opportunity for a new job," Michelle smiled. Carol was once again impressed with Michelle's answer. Tip (honesty is the best policy).

"We do have a great package for family leave, Michelle. Tell me, what was the most challenging thing you ever faced in your last job and how did you handle it?" Carol leaned forward. This interview is going well.

"Thanks, for asking that question, Carol," Michelle stated. She continued, "It happened when the power went out and the office panicked. I was working late that day. I knew I had to think on my feet. The calls stopped coming in so, I pressed a key that routed all incoming calls directly to voicemail. Following desk rules, I reached for the office's *Standard Operating Procedures guide,* (SOP); and found the answers in the emergency section. As it was layed out in the manual, I used the Intercom to inform the office power was down. I advised them not to panic. I told them I contacted the designated generator host. Next, in precision with operational procedures, I located our generator supply. Nance oversaw the electrical components, when the on-site electrician was not there. I called Nance, using his number from the emergency directory. I used my cell phone. Within twenty-minutes Nance arrived. Soon, our power was up. The next day, I received a lot of high-fives and smiles. Later, I received a commendation from the company, for a job well done. To me, I was simply doing my job. I was glad things worked out, to the benefit for the company and all," Michelle smiled. Mrs. Mitchell was so impressed with Michelle's answers tears welled in her eyes. It appeared that Michelle was just the person Carol had been looking for. Michelle read, *"Employee's Only."* She was well-prepared for her interview!

"Well, when would you be able to begin employment, Michelle?" a happy Carol Mitchell asked, the very proud Michelle.

"It's up to the company's needs," Michelle answered back. When the interview was over, Michelle asked the interviewer if there was anything else, she wanted to know about her to Carol's no.

The interview went well. Afterwards, Carol told her secretary to clear her calendar and let the other candidates know she made her choice. She was set to hire Michelle. When you look at this interview, one sees how well-prepared Michelle was for this interview. She was spontaneous with her answers. She was honest about her home situation with her mother. She knew the company in advance because she had done her research the night before at the public library. She proved to be a good employee, who was resourceful and could think on her feet. Michelle was exactly what *Company A* was hoping to find in their next employee.

What to do after the interview is over

After the interveiw was over, Michelle asked her husband to stop at a convenience store to get a thank you card for Carol. She filled out the card and, she had her husband driver her to the post office to mail it ensuring that the card would arrive to Carol the next day. No matter how many times you interview, always send a polite thank you card to the interviewer. Cards are available reasonably at convenience and dollar stores.

Your Job References

The night before her interview, Michelle called all six of her references. Only one was not available to give her a reference, because they moved out of the country. Feeling great about her interview the previous day, Michelle let her references know that they might be getting a call for a reference from *Company A*.

Two days later, after Carol received the thank you card, she called Michelle to tell the happy young lady she got the job!

The Offer Letter - What to Say

In Michelle's interview she mentioned her aging mother was the reason she didn't move to another state with her previous company. Because she did well in the interview, and the offer letter is in the mail, this is a great time for Michelle to negotiate family leave options for her mother. When such negotiations take place from inception, it will clear up any future discrepancies, in the event Michelle would have to take family leave to care for her ailing mother. Getting such clarity up front creates a great opportunity for the employer and the employee to communicate about availability and future availability as it pertains to family leave. The offer letter is a great way to get the kind of pay and benefits you know your valued experience is worth.

Know your value and worth and the importance of asking for what you deserve. Now, is the best time to seek all the things you deserve in your new job!

How to prepare for the first day of work

Michelle negotiated her family leave time during the Offer letter negotiations through *Company A's* Human Resources Department and then she signed on the dotted line. The negotiations worked out well for her because she understood her value as a new employee and was not afraid to negotiate a great deal for and her family. She read this book, "Employee's Only." She knew that it's when you're first hired that you have your strongest bargaining power, with a new company. Also, clarifying her family in advance gives both sides time to plan for Michelle's temporary worker during such family leave needs. Now, Michelle is ready to go to orientation for her new job. Both sides have the potential to work well together forevermore when communicating well from the beginning is key. After orientation, Michelle will begin her first day on the job. Congratulations to Michelle Wood.

End of Chapter Refresher

1. Be on time for the interview

2. Negotiate the offer letter

3. Be ready to answer questions honestly

4. Be confident

5. Dress well for you job interview

6. Get plenty of rest for the interview

Chapter 9

Organize Your Office?

You have done a lot of work to get the job, and you must get off to a running start. One way to do this is by being organized. After training, Michelle wanted to organize her office to suit her needs so she could be most efficient in her new front office role. She did it mostly at home through the company's shared files system after she was issued clearance via email to get on board. She organized the structure of the company from the CEO down to the janitor and during this time Michelle made a commitment to learn everyone's name on the directory including regular vendors. She created a cheat sheet so if someone called asking for one of these names, she would be spontaneous in her response because she still had to get familiar with the many names in the company directory.

How to win without asking questions

When a company hires you, they're looking for people that can sustain without a lot of direction and questions. Michelle knew this in advance. A few days before the previous receptionist retired, Michelle watched her closely. She asked questions and took notes for the entire introduction. Michelle aimed to function in the same manner that *Company A* was used to, she'd not change too much, other than to optimize efficiency in her new Front Desk Receptionist role. The only thing she did was organize new files, but she decided if it was not broken there was no need to change things, especially since Gracie had been with the company for thirty-years. At her retirement party yesterday, she said she was leaving because of retirement purposes and to travel. The transition worked out well. At the end of the day, Gracie was glad to leave knowing that Michelle was keeping things the same as they had been before.

Alert: Avoid Gossip/Office Cliques

Naturally, anyone who lands a new job is happy and you want everyone to know. The one thing you want to do is talk! Be careful, though. The first week during Michelle's employment she noticed there were some busy bodies with a lot of bad things to say about certain people in the company, including Gracie who was already gone. One of the things Michelle researched before taking the job was how to stay out of the office cliques and be polite at the same time. Here are some tips on dealing with office gossips!

- Listen and be quiet

- Stay Neutral…Don't pick sides

- Don't talk about politics or religion

- Be humble…I am busy, must get back to work

- Be polite…Excuse yourself to go back to work

- Stay busy so you don't have time to answer idiotic gossip

Michelle learned to listen and smile and get on with her work in the smartest manner. Taking sides, or talking about others on the job, religion or politics, can be a losing concept that one should never engage in on the job. Michelle was on a 90-day probationary period and she needed to stay clean. She was fully aware to be careful with those who liked to gossip on the job and do an outstanding job!

What about Temporary Employment?

I don't want to be the bearer of bad news so, here is the good news about Temporary Employment. The minute you begin earning money for the agency and for the client, you are entitled to the same remedies in law as a full-time employee. So long as you can prove that you are essential in some way of creating earnings for either or both entities. Temporary officers will skirt the issues when there is trouble on one of their client's sites, because they want to be the ones solely to resolve, and or mitigate your issues. But when one considers the nuts and bolts of it, if your rights are violated on the job under Title VII of the Civil Rights Act or your statutory rights are violated in any ways under the law, both companies will bear the responsibilities. Try as they may, not to tell you such, remember this. If you are the victim of sexual harassment at a client's site, the client is responsible with your agency. Hence, they can both be held responsible for a statutory violation that happens on the job. Remember the statute of limitations in filing a case, get an attorney. Hopefully it will not come to that, but it does not hurt for you to know your rights on the job.

Chapter 10

Your Rights, Temporary

As we stipulated in the, as a Temporary, Contingent or Contract worker, you have the same rights as permanent employees to not be discriminated against in the American workplace. Neither the agency nor the Contract Company where you work can discriminate against you because of your race, sex, religion, color, national origin, age or disability. Both the agency you work for and the company that they send you to share responsibility for making sure that you are not exposed to illegal discrimination and this is worth repeating because of the exigency of the situation and the limited time parameters some states have for you to file a case.

despite laws that protect all workers, many temporary workers face illegal discrimination in the workplace and are told, (usually by the "agency," to address problems with the agency only). It is important for temporary workers to know their rights fully and, these workers need to be able to demand the respect that they deserve on the job.

Am I a Temporary Worker?

You are a temporary employee if you are employed by a temporary employment agency and they place you at another company's work place. In this case, both the agency staff and the management staff may supervise you where they send you to work. In the scheme of things, you are contracted out to another company. You can tell by whose being in charge, the agency or the company where you work who is the boss. As a temporary worker, it is safe to assume that both the agency and the company that you are sent to are your bosses. In order to gauge further, who is ultimately responsible for you as a temporary worker, ascertain who is supplying the fundamental tools, materials or equipment that you are going to work with. How are you paid? Do you receive benefits? Since there may be many other factors that can render you to be a temporary worker, call the ERA or other organizations to find out more information about your temporary employment status.

Remember: If you are discriminated against as a temporary worker, the responsibility may fall on both the agency that employs you and the company they sent you to work for. The agency should stop the discrimination. In addition, the company they send you to may be responsible if they are supervising your work; if they have control over you during your interim assignment. Ask yourself if the agency and the company both share or split duties.

Remember: If things go wrong on your assignment, you have the right to go through your agency's complaint process. Write down the complaint. Next, complain to both companies. File a charge against the temporary agency and the place where they sent you to work with a state or federal agency.

Follow the same rules that the regular fully employed worker does when filing your state or federal claim. Talk with an employment lawyer to acquire more information on exercising your full rights. People who implement these laws as a working professional have a better understanding of how you can legally pursue your rights. Like the regular full-time employee, remember, document your case, and keep copious records. Maintain a paper trail of work events. Always use the company's complaint or grievance process to resolve any problems you may experience on the job. You can call ERA'S advice and counseling line at 1-800-839-4ERA for more information regarding your temporary employee rights. For attorneys call: 404-(521-0777).

How to handle conflict on the job

Everyone wants to be happy on the job, produce and prosper. Sometimes things will happen in the course of a day's work, and all employees must be equipped with how to handle conflict on the job in ways that garner fairness for all involved. Rule #1 never fight on the job.

1. Don't use profanity on the job
2. Don't drink on the job
3. Don't wear offensive clothes/hats to the job
4. Be the first to resolve issues on the job
5. Be sure to memorialize times/dates of office conflict

End of Chapter Refresher

1. Stay out of office cliques
2. Know your rights as a temporary worker

Chapter 11

Human Resources

What is the Human Resources Department?

The Human Resources Department is a great place for the employee to learn about benefits on the job. However, many employees have little knowledge of all that the Human Resources Department can do. This needs to be your first contact for conflict on the job. This is where all employment records are maintained. Generally, if your employer evaluates your job performance, The Human Resources Department is where all employment records are maintained, so whatever materials are given to you, make copies and always render a response to the HR Department's communications. Here is more on what the Human Resources Department can do.

The Human Resources person develops and administers HR plans and procedures for all personnel. This person organizes and controls essentially all activities of the department and participates in developing departmental goals, objectives and systems with assistance to the corporate executives in the company. Employment laws guide this person strictly. In common words: The Human Resources Manager has a powerful influence in the company and she or he maintain imminent power in settling employment and money issues with you more swiftly really than anyone else in the company. Presidents, and company vice presidents, do not want to deal with run-of-the mill problems that can be resolved below their level. A good HR person has excellent bargaining knowledge, and superb resolution skills. This person does not want conflict to expand beyond the parameters of the company.

The Human Resources Manager, updates compensation programs, and rewrites job descriptions as necessary; conducts annual salary surveys and develops merit pool (salary budgets). This person is the most prominent guide you must get your point across to, in middle and upper management. *Find out who the HR person is and if you want to take them to Starbucks one day, that would be a great strategic move on your part.* Seriously, she/he controls personnel policies, procedures and they regularly update the employee handbook manuals. It never hurts for the HR person to know first hand what a great employee you are. If you have a question regarding any of your employment rights, it is the HR person's job to have or get the answers for you. Generally, the Human Resources Department maintains all affirmative action program; files the annual EEO-1; in conformance with state and federal regulations.

How to write winning letters

If conflict is not settled correctly in the Human Resources Department, you need to know the cadence of writing letters and how factual notes and materials will amicably resolve your case. When you are writing an important letter to the Human Resources Department about wages, or conflict on the job, be mindful of how it can be used later for or against you in a court of law. Therefore, brevity is important and knowing how to write a letter to the Human Resources Department is essential. One key thing to know is keep it brief. On the next page, you're going to find the sample letter Michelle wrote to the Human Resources Department. This proves why an employee must maintain copies of Offer Letters to prove promises that were made, especially after the person that made the promise has moved on from the company. Remember to check your personnel file at least once every six months to see if it reflects the true events of your employment. Managers don't intend to lose things, but it does happen sometimes. That's why you must be the first protector of you. Remember Michelle's amazing interview? Following is her letter to the Human Resources Department, about Family Leave.

Carol Denise Mitchell

Sample letter to the Human Resources Department

Dear Company A: Date: January 01, 20_____

    My name is Michelle Wood. I have been working as a receptionist for *Company A* for one year and was hired by Carol Mitchell. In June of this year, I requested 3 family days off to care for my ailing mother and was denied. I have attached my old offer letter to prove that your former *Human Resources Manager, Carol Mitchell* approved this leave, pursuant to the fact, that I request the time off one week in advance, and I did, but Sandra Smith denied my request.

  .   Thanks, for looking at the (attached) letter, proving my statement. I look forward to resolving this issue with you as soon as possible. Thank you for giving me an answer by this Friday, at 5:00PM.

Yours's truly,

Michelle Wood

Front Desk Receptionist/Mail

Problem solved - Just the facts please!

Turns out that when Carol Mitchell took another job a few months after she hired Michelle, she had not given The Human Resources Department the signed copy of Michelle's offer letter that included her family leave promissory approval. The new Human Resources Manager, honored Michelle's letter, which was dated back to when she was hired. Because Michelle read "Employee's Only," Michelle was able to get results for her conflict sooner than she expected, because her evidentiary officer letter was very clear!

End of Chapter Refresher

1. Maintain facts, times, dates, witnesses

2. Keep, file all correspondence

3. Don't get aggressive; get the facts

4. Write a short concise letter

5. Be kind, be patient and confident

6. Consider the letter a demand and specify an expectation date for resolution.

Chapter 12

The Employee Handbook

Importance of the Employee Handbook

Now, that we're learning how to handle things that pop up on the job, please know this. The Employee Handbook is your bible. It is the one most important thing you will ever receive on the job and it's the first thing a lawyer will want to see to defend an employee dispute on the job. This book includes a lot of material. It outlines the company's mission statement, promises, and its Standard Operations Procedures and is carefully written in the interest of the employer. Here are some topics you will see in this handbook:

Important information you may find in the employee Handbook are geared towards the employer's interest in avoiding potential lawsuits:

1. Family Medical Leave Materials

2. EEOC Discrimination Policies

3. Worker's Compensation Policies

4. Sexual Harassment Guidelines/Tutorials

5. Cautious being told the handbook is not a contract/it can be depending on what's in it.

6. Paid time off and other policy

7. Pay/Promotions and Benefits

Each employee that is hired directly by a company will get and or receive an Employee Handbook. Keep it. Read every word of this book. Follow it religiously. If something goes wrong on the job, make sure that the specific details in this manual match the companies stated expectations of you. The manual will talk about time cards, pay, the Human Resources Department and how to access company information via a shared outlet that you will get more information about once you're fully hired and are vested in the company. For temporary workers, this book is also important too. Though temps may not get a copy of the employment handbook like a regular employee will, but some of the things entailed in this book pertains to Temporary Employee's as well. Generally, the Employee Handbook will detail how to resolve in house problems.

You will be referred to the Human Resources Department. This book will also mention a said policy against Sexual Harassment or discrimination on the job. Chances are if conflict can't be resolved within the company, an employeee will exert their rights to go outside of the company to a state or government agency to handle problems. The Human Resources Department will make a stipulation citing that an employee must attempt to remedy conflict in house first before going outside to a government or state agency. Keep in mind, as an employee you must follow the Employee Handbook Guidelines specifically. If the Handbook stipulates that *Company A* had thirty-days to resolve conflict before you can file with a state or government agency, *you must abide by this guideline*. If you usurp this process, no matter how sound your case is you may lose in court because you signed the Employee Handbook, and you did not follow the in-house procedural guide down to the letter, before taking your dispute to an outside agency. If you have followed the letter of the law per the Employment Handbook and resolution has not been resolved within the company's time parameter, here's what you must do. Write a letter, as follows:

<u>About your letter</u>

1. Present facts only, date letter accordingly

2. Keep the letter short/concise

3. Attach information that proves your point

4. Don't get mean or nasty in the letter

5. Always mention a time frame for a response

6. Mail the letter by certified mail

Sample Letter to the Human Resources Department

Dear Company, Ae   January 01, 20_____

    My name is Fred. I have been working as an IT Manager for your company for five-years with no problems. I was promised a promotion by Carol Mitchell that was supposed to take place two months ago. And, unexpected to many, she quit a few months ago perhaps forgetting about my promotion. I have an email stating that I'd get that promotion during my last employment evaluation, which was very positive. To that end, my wife and I recently purchased a home so, I was truly in need of the raise Carol said goes with the promotion. I followed your guidelines per the Employment Handbook and thirty-days have passed to no consequences on your part.

    It says the following in Company A's Handbook. *"If your conflict is not resolved by email or letter within thirty-days, you're free to seek remedy outside of this process."* Well, it's been 33 days since I was due for the promotion. I'd still prefer resolving this issue in-house because I don't care to file a complaint with the EEOC or the DEFH. Should I not hear back from you within 5 working days, I will seek to be made whole elsewhere.

Sincerely,

Fred Diamond

ASCP IT Manager, Floor (A)

Fred Diamond's letter was strictly written. It was perfect. Fred adhered to Company A policy, per the handbook, therefore remediation was his immediately. Apparently, Carol left many loose ends unresolved when she left *Company (A)*. Fred's promotion was one of them. Like Michelle, Fred read the Company Handbook. He followed the Human Resources Department request down to the letter and gave Company A an additional 3-days to atone to his demand. The reason this is important is because when you follow the company's own mission statement, it's very difficult for them to defend against you in court. Fred wrote a short, concise letter. He stipulated how he preferred to handle his promotion issue(s) in house. Fred cited the number of days he had to handle his conflict before he was entitled to handle it via an outside agency. The Human Resources took no time at all in handling Fred's issues. He was given the promotion with back pay.

Lesson's-Learned

In most professional work environments, they're not out to get you. It's your job to keep track of your rights on the job. If promises are made have the proof to fight back or to prove what is owed to you like Michelle and Fred did. Never throw anything away as it pertains to your employment at a company. *"Always, write things down."* You never know when you're going to have to prove something with dates, times and other evidence. It's nothing personal other than the fact that we're working with humans. Humans make mistakes. One thing I have learned over the years is this. If you are telling the truth and you can supply the facts, you're going to win each time. Don't ever make things up to suit an erroneous purpose of advancing yourself at someone else's expense. Conflicts aren't always handled as easily as described above. Each case is different. Make sure if you're going outside of the company for remedy, that your case is honest and leveled on facts that you can prove and, let the Human Resources Department know of your intentions, so they can try to remedy the matter, first. Always keep company emails, voicemails and that awesome Employment Handbook.

How to answer your first evaluation

If you're reading *"Employee's Only,"* you're well informed by now! Being a good employment helped Fred get a promotion he was promised and here's why. Each employee should work hard on the job. Annually some jobs will evaluate such a performance to determine if you qualify for more benefits or a raise. This is a very important time in your employment. Suffice it to say, whomever is evaluating your work performance may not know the full breadth of what you bring to the job. Some job classifications are far reaching. You're told you're going to be doing one thing; and, invariably you may end up doing a lot more. Instead of placing your job in jeopardy by complaining, write down all the things you're doing for the job with times, dates and witnesses. Once your employment evaluation is issued to you, always be prepared to write a quantifiable answer. Add additional sheets of paper if you must. Your answer to an employment evaluation is essential. All your written evaluations will be routed to the Human Resources Department and will be placed in your file. Practice due diligence, it's your right to add value to your job performances. Add a few pages to this evaluation as your basement to this evaluation whether the outcome is good or bad.

<u>Important tips:</u>

1. The evaluation will be kept in your personnel file

2. Its vital for you to answer an evaluation to add your input

3. If you disagree – explain why

4. Feel free to ask for explanation, when rating is not clear

5. Use this as an opportunity to clarify your work input.

The Human Resources Manager does a lot more than file department records and conduct new employee orientations. This is the most important resource you should know in the company. Therefore, it will not hurt you to learn who this person is and make them your strongest work alliance.

The Human Resources person develops and administers HR plans and procedures for all personnel. This person organizes and controls essentially all activities of the department and participates in developing departmental goals, objectives and systems with assistance to the corporate executives in the company. Employment laws guide this person strictly. In common words: The Human Resources Manager has a powerful influence in the company and she or she maintain imminent power in settling employment and money issues with you more swiftly really than anyone else in the company. Presidents, and Company vice presidents, do not want to deal with run of the mill problems that can be resolved below their level. A good HR person has excellent bargaining knowledge, and superb resolution skills.

The Human Resources Manager, updates compensation programs, and rewrites job descriptions as necessary; conducts annual salary surveys and develops merit pool (salary budgets). This person is the most prominent guide for you when you must get your point across to middle and upper management. Seriously, she/he controls personnel policies, procedures and they regularly update the employee handbook manuals and it will never hurt for the HR person to know first hand what a great employee you are. If you have a question regarding any of your employment rights, it is the HR person's job to have or get the answers for you. Generally, the Human Resources Department maintains all affirmative action program; files the annual EEO-1; in conformance with state and federal regulations.

Knowing Your Time-Card

SAMPLE COMPANY TIME-CARD

It is consequential for you to keep track of all hours worked, regular and overtime. Audit and store all your work check stubs and or reports. Double check regular time, training time for a new job, overtime, and determine if double-time is recorded correctly on *EACH* time card record. Make sure your deductions are correct. Add and subtract your totals to make sure you are being paid accurately for all time worked.

Practice your math, until you are confident that you understand your check stub. Under California Labor Code §§ 226-226.6; Industrial Relations your check should contain the following information:

CA Labor Code § 226.6 (2017)

Any employer who knowingly and intentionally violates the provisions of Section 226, or any officer, agent, employee, fiduciary, or other person who has the control, receipt, custody, or disposal of, or pays, the wages due any employee, and who knowingly and intentionally participates or aids in the violation of any provision of Section 226 is guilty of a misdemeanor and, upon conviction thereof, shall be fined not more than one thousand dollars ($1,000) or be imprisoned not to exceed one year, or both, at the discretion of the court. That fine or imprisonment, or both, shall be in addition to any other penalty provided by law.

- Gross wages earned
- Total amount of hours worked
- All Deductions
- Net wages earned
- Date you were paid for including month, day and year
- Social Security number
- Name and Address of the employer
- Number of piece rates units earned

Chapter 13

Sexual Harassment/Extensively

Because sexual harassment can be costly to the victim and the employer, in *"Employee's Only"* we want to leave no doubt how important this topic is. Let it be said in no uncertain terms that Sexual Harassment is against the law. The day you begin your new job read the employee manual. Next learn what the company policy is on harassment and sexual harassment. REMEMBER: It is your right to say no to a person that pursues you on the job. Many companies have stringent policies against sexual harassment. Consult your Employee Handbook to find out what the policy is and hold the company accountable to their written policy regarding sexual harassment. Remember to report harassment, and sexual harassment ***immediately*** to your supervisor. Tell the harasser to cease and desist. (See the sample cease and desist letter to the offender below.) All employees are entitled to work in an environment that is free of harassment.

Types of Sexual Harassment

Types of Harassment: Types of Harassment California Law defines the following types of harassment Verbal Harassment – Epithets, derogatory comments or slurs Physical Harassment – Assault, impeding or blocking movement, or any physical interference with normal work or movement, when directed at an individual Visual Harassment – Derogatory posters, calendars, cartoons or drawings

Sexual Favors – Unwanted sexual advances which condition an employment benefit upon an exchange of sexual favors Gender Harassment – Due to pregnancy, childbirth or related medical conditions

Quid Pro Quo: Quid Pro Quo Quid Pro Quo: Quid pro quo sexual harassment occurs when an individual's submission to or rejection of sexual advances or conduct of a sexual nature is used as the basis for employment decisions affecting the individual or the individual's submission to such conduct is made a term or condition of employment. It is sufficient to show a threat of economic loss to prove quid pro quo sexual harassment. A single sexual advance may constitute harassment if it is linked to the granting or denial of employment benefits. Courts have held employers strictly liable for quid pro quo sexual harassment initiated by supervisory employees. A subordinate who submits and then changes her or his mind and refuses can still bring quid pro quo sexual harassment charges.
Hostile Environment: Hostile Environment Hostile Environment: Hostile environment sexual harassment occurs when unwelcome sexual conduct unreasonably interferes with an individual's job performance or creates a hostile, intimidating or offensive work environment even though the harassment may not result in tangible or economic job consequences, that is, the person may not lose pay or a promotion. There are two conditions that determine liability for employers in cases of hostile environment sexual harassment: The employer knew or should have known about the harassment, and The employer failed to take appropriate

Chapter 14

Worker's Compensation II

If you are injured on the job, chances are you are going to be confused by the complicated process of *Workers Compensation law*. You are going to want to know what the process is. Even if your injury was a total acccident, chances are after you get hurt on the job your relationship at work will change. One way or another it will not be the same. Workers who are hurt are sometimes confused by the procedures.

Be sure: That you have a case and pursue your benefits fully. Look in the yellow pages for a Workers Compensation attorney. Familiarize your-self with each detail of what your case entails:

Temporary Disability

TD is paid at a weekly rate during the time the doctor says that the injured worker is unable to work because of the injury. TD is paid at the rate of two-thirds (66%) of the injured employees gross earnings up to the maximum that is set by law. The maximum rate for Temporary Disability is presently paid at the rate of $490.00 a week, *(see chart on the next page for additional rates)* for injuries that have occurred on or after January 01, 1996. Wait for first check: two-weeks.

Permanent Disability For workers left with any residual disability they may be entitled to receive a *permanent disability award*. These monies are not payable until the medical condition becomes permanent and stationary, which means the physcian has signed off on the condition as having been leveled off and will stay substantially the same in the future. Remember: If the doctor says there has been a total recovery, there would be no permanent disability award.

Note: *When dealing with Workers Compensation issues and or injuries, be smart. What may not hurt today, may sear tomorrow. If injured on the job, always negotiate for future medical awards for your injury where it is warranted. Get an attorney!*

Medical Consultation

When the doctor ends your treatment and says that your medical condition may be permanent and stationary or that you can go back to work, get examined by a Qualified Medical Examiner. If you are not represented by an attorney, the insurance Company will send you the injured party, a list of doctors, (QME) to choose from. If you, the injured worker have a lawyer, your lawyer will choose the QME or make an agreement with the insurance Company to utilize QME.

Settlement of the Case

When all the medical reports are submitted with a detail narrative including professional opinions by all of your treating doctors, you may be ready to settle your case. The report will be rated and a percentage of disability will be assigned to the doctors opinions in accordance with the rating guidelines of the State of California. The rating percentage is then converted into a monetary settlement amount and all ratings and preset rating guidelines are arranged in accordance with a schedule.

Note: *If you have been without an attorney before; now is the time to hire one. You will receive more of the benefits you deserve if you have an experienced lawyer*

Worker's Compensation Part II

Permanent Disability

For workers left with any residual disability they may be entitled to receive a *permanent disability award*. These monies are not payable until the medical condition becomes permanent and stationary, which means the physcian has signed off on the condition as having been leveled off and will stay substantially the same in the future. Remember: If the doctor says there has been a total recovery, there would be no permanent disability award.

Note: *When dealing with Workers Compensation issues and or injuries, be smart. What may not hurt today, may sear tomorrow. If injured on the job, always negotiate for future medical awards for your injury where it is warranted.*

Medical Consultation

When the doctor ends your treatment and says that your medical condition may be permanent and stationary or that you can go back to work, get examined by a Qualified Medical Examiner. If you are not represented by an attorney, the insurance Company will send you the injured party, a list of doctors, (QME) to choose from. If you, the injured worker have a lawyer, your lawyer will choose the QME or make an agreement with the insurance Company to utilize QME.

Settlement of the Case

When all the medical reports are submitted with a detail narrative including professional opinions by all of your treating doctors, you may be ready to settle your case. The report will be rated and a percentage of disability will be assigned to the doctors opinions in accordance with the rating guidelines of the State of California. The rating percentage is then converted into a monetary settlement amount and all ratings and preset rating guidelines are arranged in accordance with a schedule.

Note: *If you have been without an attorney before; now is the time to hire one. You will receive more of the benefits you deserve if you have an experienced lawyer to negotiate your case for you. Consult the State of California Bar Association or your yellow pages for a Workers Compensation Attorney.*

Rehabilitation

If you are not able to return to the job you had when you got injured; you may be eligible for rehabilitation. While you are pursuing rehabilitation training you will continue to receive either temporary disability benefits or a rehabilitation maintenance allowance.

Workers' Compensation Appeals Board

The Workers' Compensation Appeals Board is the state court for all industrial injuries involving your employer. The proceedings are administrative and there are not juries. Contact an-office in your city for more information regarding your rights in Civil Court.

Important Points to Remember

If you are hurt on the job, no matter how minor it is, report it <u>immediately</u>, and demand, to see a doctor right away. An injury or illness that takes place due to your job is a workers' compensation injury or illness. If somebody tells you, "well, you picked up that box the wrong way! Had you picked it up right, you would not have gotten hurt." Say thank you to that person, then march right over to the telephone, call the HR person, tell them that you were hurt, and tell them to please send you all forms from BC to present for your injury. If there are witnesses that saw you get hurt <u>never,</u> feel embarrassed to write that person's name down or ask them to sign a declaration, and look up at the clock and right down the time you were hurt.

If they don't testify today because of fear, or out of losing their job; believe me, they will have to talk when you subpoena them later to come to the Worker's Compensation Appeals Board for adjudication of your claim. Honest employers recognize injuries, and they process such matters accordingly. But, remember:

"If you get hurt on the job, no matter how minor, tell somebody immediately."

Worker's Compensation Part III

Rehabilitation

If you are not able to return to the job you had when you got injured; you may be eligible for rehabilitation. While you are pursuing rehabilitation training you will continue to receive either temporary disability benefits or a rehabilitation maintenance allowance.

Workers' Compensation Appeals Board

The Workers' Compensation Appeals Board is the state court for all industrial injuries involving your employer. The proceedings are administrative and there are not juries. Contact a office in your city for more information regarding your rights in Civil Court.

Important Points to Remember

If you are hurt on the job, no matter how minor it is, report it immediately, and demand, to see a doctor right away. An injury or illness that takes place due to your job is a workers' compensation injury or illness. If somebody tells you, "well, you picked up that box the wrong way! Had you picked it up right, you would not have gotten hurt." Say thank you to that person, then march right over to the telephone, call the HR person, tell them that you were hurt, and tell them to please send you all forms from BC to present for your injury. If there are witnesses that saw you get hurt never, feel embarrassed to write that person's name down or ask them to sign a declaration, and look up at the clock and right down the time you were hurt. If they don't testify today because of fear, or out of losing their job; believe me, they will have to talk when you subpoena them later to come to the Worker's Compensation Appeals Board for adjudication of your claim. Honest employers recognize injuries, and they process such matters accordingly. Workers Compensation Attorneys are very busy. Your case is important to them. Therefore, please be considerate and keep in mind before calling about your case incessantly, see if you can handle some questions yourself first.

<u>Listen to your Worker's Compensation Attorney</u>

1. I may not always be readily available

2. You are not my only client

3. I am at the board, a hearing or a conference OR adjudicating another case

4. Your case is complicated to you; but, not to me

5. You can call the insurance company yourself about your check

6. You can call the insurance company yourself to change a doctor's appointment

7. Call doctors (directly) to change appointment dates/times

8. Do not sign anything without my advice

Chapter 15

Important Sample Letters Section

SAMPLE CEASE AND DESIST LETTER TO OFFENDER

January 5, 200_____

John Doe, CEO

XXXX

Mr John Doe:

On January 02, 20_____ I told you that I was not interested in you. After work, on the aforementioned date you pulled up to the bus stop at 5:30 p.m. demanding that I get into the car with you. When I refused, you got out of your car. Next, you approached me. When I said I was going to call the police you left. John, this is harassment. I find your actions extremely troublesome and offensive.

According to Company A's Sexual Harassment policy, page 23 of the manual, I must give you this cease and desist letter, before filing with an outside agency. Therefore, for the second time I am asking you to stop, cease, and desist. If you contact me or stalk me again, I will report you to the police and to your supervisor, until these actions stop. Furthermore, I can exercise my opportunities with the EEOC and, DEFH if these actions continue, and don't stop at once.

Carol Denise Mitchell

Sample Letter Two

SAMPLE LAST LETTER TO EMPLOYER

BEFORE FILING WITH OUTSIDE AGENCIES

CERTIFIED MAIL/EMAIL

Attn: President, Yoo

P.O. Box XXX

Los Angeles, California 90210

Dear Mr. Yoo:

I have completed the following actions in accordance with your grievance policy as stated on pages 35 & 36 of your *Employee Handbook*:

- I reported discrimination to my supervisor the day it happened on 11/30/23.

- On 12/18/23 I appropriately submitted your form #CS92-05 to Kathy Doe in the Department of Human Resources.

- On 12/07/, I met with you. Then on 01/11/ (the date you said you would get back to me), I heard nothing from you. On that date, Kathy said you ended my employment without cause.

To date, I have followed your complaint process according to policy as stated in the Employee Handbook, page 28 down to the letter. Still, my grievance has been overlooked and has not been settled.

I sincerely want to resolve these issues in house. Please contact me at 310-565-XXXX in five-days to discuss resolution of the wrongful termination, loss of overtime wages and other employment issues. Otherwise, on January 24, 2023, I will carry my petition to the *Department of Labor* and the *Department of Fair Employment & Housing* and *the Equal Employment Opportunity Commission*, where I am sure I will get fair resolution of my discrimination issues and wage losses, et al.

Sample Letter Three

THE SAMPLE DEMAND LETTER

XYZ Company

Attn: Department of Human Resources

1258 Employment Drive

Pomona, CA 91768

RE: EMPLOYMENT DISCRIMINATION, 02/12/23 - 05/05/23

Dear Department of Human Resources:

 Per our discussion, please review the attached e-mail sent to me by a witness with no interest in my case, who was also discriminated against by Guy B at XYZ Company in Pomona, CA as I was. Please review the attached letter and the initial itemization of all incidences of harassment and all expenses that were submitted to your legal department for denouement of this employment conflict.

 Before going to the Department of Fair Employment & Housing, I would like to initiate a chance to settle the case with you. I believe that the full and total sum of *$10,000.00* would be an equitable and fair settlement amount for all that I have suffered, *(see attached itemized list)* and to cover outstanding medical cost as has been itemized specifically on my list. In order to cure this situation and put it all behind me I pray that we can handle this employment matter out of court. Therefore, I sincerely hope that this faxed proposal for settlement will be agreeable to XYZ Company, and to the Department of Human Resources, and your legal department. If not, I have no other choice but to have a lawyer pursue this case further.

Demand Letter (Continued)...

Your expeditious reply to this _Settlement Proposal_ is greatly appreciated. Should I not hear from you in ten (10) working business days, then I will have no choice but to pursue and implement all my legal options fully.

Sincerely,

Jane Doe

P.O. Box XXX

Pomona, CA 91768

Sample Letter 4

Get the Cover Letter Right!

XYZ Company

P.O. Box XYZ

San Ramon, California 94583

RE: Administrative Assistant Position

<u>In Discovery Lab - Job Number 66678</u>

Dear Department of Human Resources:

 Attached, please find my resume for the *Administrative Assistant position* you advertised on your career-site today. I am seeking a versatile position chronicling the same core administrative duties that you outlined in your magnificent ad.

 Upon review of my resume, you will see that attention to detail, and excellent organization are standard operations of which I have consistently demonstrated throughout my administrative career. As a mánager, I worked well independently, as well as with others in a team setting. Overall, I truly believe that my professional skills match up perfect to what you are seeking in an administrative assistant. Therefore, I submit to you my resume with the hope that I will meet with you soon to further discuss my professional abilities.

 Here is thanking you advance for considering me for this great employment opportunity! I will follow-up with a telephone call soon to find out the status of this great career position

Sample Letter 5

SMART JOB OFFER LETTER

Mrs. Jane E. Doe

715 Greater Street - Apartment #16

San Francisco, CA 94110

Dear Ms. Doe:

    This is to confirm our nuncupative conversation regarding our offer of new employment with New Starts Company (NSC). We are pleased that you have accepted the position of Assistant Manager, at the New Starts Company Headquarters, and we look forward to working with you here.

    Your cash remuneration shall be $11.00 per hour, starting today. You will work (forty hours per week), full-time, Monday through Friday from 8:00 a.m. to 5:00 p.m. *(or as determined),* with one hour off each day for lunch. You will report to the New Starts Academy, located at 3456 XXOO Drive, in the Presidio of San Francisco. Your immediate supervisor will be Mr. XYX.

    You will be placed on probation for an introductory period of 180 days, starting your first day of work. After 90-days of full-time employment, you will be eligible for New Start's group health insurance and 401k plan with coverage starting the first day of the month following the 90-day probationary period.

    Your employment is at-will. Therefore, during your employment, you are free to leave New Start's Company at any time for any reason and NSC reserves a similar right. Thus, employment with the Company is not for a specified term and is therefore at the mutual consent of the employee and the Company.

    On behalf of New Starts, welcome to the position of Assistant Manager. Please sign this letter below to acknowledge your acceptance of the offer.

Sample Letter Five

<u>Simple Resignation Letter</u>

To Whom It May Concern:

Per our discussion of May 5, 2---- I will resign my position as Manager of the ***Hotel Maximum*** on May 12, 2----.

Those being said, please accept this note as my official employment resignation.

Allow me to take a moment to say thank you to Gosling Investors, and Mr. Doe Winifred, for having allowed me this great five-year career opportunity.

Sincerely,

Jane Doe

29XXX Fruit Tree Way

Concord, CA 94520

Carol Denise Mitchell

Let's talk Personnel Records

Employee access to personnel records

Your personnel records are the property of the employer. Check state law because federal law does not require the employer to give employees access to their personnel file. If you are a federal employee and have an issue regarding your rights and obligations of union, management and employees in a federal workplace represented by a labor union, contact the **Federal Labor Relations Authority** (FLRA) at http://www.flra.gov/. For other employees, all files should only contain job-related information, documentation. At least twenty states including California, Illinois and Massachusetts do let employees into their files. Ask to see the contents of your personnel file regularly in writing, at least twice a year. Be prepared to make copies of this file and literally defend anything in that file that is unfamiliar and outlandish to you.

Federal contractors are required to maintain any personnel or employment records made or kept by the contractor.

Examples of records that must be maintained:

- Job descriptions
- Job postings and advertisements
- Records of job offers
- Applications and resumes
- Interview notes

- Tests and test results

- Written employment policies and procedures

- Personnel files

Inside tip: Employers may not want you to have your file if the information in the file will be used to support a legal claim against the Company. Keep your own records to match whatever grievances or conflict your employer may try to boast against you. Ask for copies of everything. If your name is on it, get a copy. Preserve it. If the information contained on work documents is not true or correct, dispute it immediately, *(in writing)*. **Remember:** when you are in a fight against your employer, generally, the burden of proof lies with the employer. If your personal work records are as meticulous and straight as theirs are, you have an increased chance of winning your rightful claim against the employer. When the employer discovers that you know your rights, chances are they will not ride you so hard on the small things. Then, you will have time to go on and be the great employee that you are!

What *they* keep track of

- Your mistakes – each time you're given warning

- Your conflicts – each time there is a dispute.

- Your complaints – all complaints about work.

- Your work performance – all of your work evaluations.

What *you* keep track of

- Your mistakes – to justify with dates, witnesses.

- Your conflicts – to correlate your side of disputes.

- Your complaints – justified with times, dates, witnesses.

- Your work performance – attach pages to evaluations!

- Specific times dates – chronicle events in real time.

Top 50 Places to work for

2019 Top 50 Companies to Work For

Hot List! Top 50 Jobs Forbes

1. Facebook Company Rating: 4.6

2. Bain & Company Rating: 4.6

3. Boston Consulting Group Company Rating: 4.6

4. In-N-Out Burger Company Rating: 4.6

5. Google Company Rating: 4.6

6. lululemon Company Rating: 4.6

7. HubSpot Company Rating: 4.6

8. World Wide Technology Company Rating: 4.5

9. St. Jude Children's Research Hospital Company Rating: 4.5

10. Ultimate Software Company Rating: 4.5

11. SAP Company Rating: 4.5

12. McKinsey & Company Rating: 4.5

13. Keller Williams Company Rating: 4.5

14. E. & J. Gallo Winery Company Rating: 4.5

15. Salesforce Company Rating: 4.5

16. Power Home Remodeling Company Rating: 4.5

17. Delta Air Lines Company Rating: 4.5

18. Academy Mortgage Company Rating: 4.5

19. The Church of Jesus Christ of Latter-day Saints Company Rating: 4.5

20. H E B Company Rating: 4.5

21. LinkedIn Company Rating: 4.5

22. DocuSign Company Rating: 4.4

23. Southwest Airlines Company Rating: 4.4

24. NVIDIA Company Rating: 4.4

25. Fast Enterprises Company Rating: 4.4

26. AvalonBay Communities Company Rating: 4.4

27. Nestlé Purina Company Rating: 4.4

28. Blizzard Entertainment Company Rating: 4.4

29. Paylocity Company Rating: 4.4

30. Intuit Company Rating: 4.4

31. Adobe Company Rating: 4.4

32. NewYork Presbyterian Hospital Company Rating: 4.4

33. VMware Company Rating: 4.4

34. Concur Company Rating: 4.4

36. Forrester Company Rating: 4.4

37. Kimpton Hotels & Restaurants Company Rating: 4.4

38. Johnson & Johnson Company Rating: 4.4

39. Microsoft Company Rating: 4.4

40. Ellie Mae Company Rating: 4.4

41. Hilton Company Rating: 4.4

42. Yardi Systems Company Rating: 4.4

43. Smile Brands Company Rating: 4.4

44. Progressive Leasing Company Rating: 4.4

45. Memorial Sloan Kettering Company Rating: 4.4

46. Texas Health Resources Company Rating: 4.4

47. Protiviti Company Rating: 4.3

48. Oshkosh Corporation Company Rating: 4.3

49. Wegmans Food Markets Company Rating: 4.3

50. SpaceX Company Rating: 4.

Top 15 Search Engines

1. Indeed, Job Search

2. Glassdoor Jobs

3. LinkedIn

4. Google for Jobs

5. Monster

6. ZipRecruiter

7. Simply Hired

8. CareerBuilder

9. Snag (Formerly Snagajob)

10. LinkUp

11. Craigslist Jobs

12. US.jobs

13. Robert Half

14. Job.com

15. USAjobs.gov

Things to remember from Carol Mitchell

Employee in the Know

We have held you down quite nicely. If you have a job already, feel free to share this information with someone looking for a job. Employees are the biggest asset any company has. Now, that you know how to look for a job and be a good employee, be smart. Remember your rights. Know the locations of important places to go to remedy a work situation. This book is relevant to workers in every state in the union. Access the public library for more specific information on employment law as it applies to you. Remember, be professional. Be the best employee, you can possibly be. Let's take one last refresher course. That way you will not have any ambiguity on what your role is in a company. Here is wishing you happiness and job growth, all across America!

From the beginning

Now that you know your role in the workplace, understand that when you seek out a company for employment, you are asking them to entrust you to be a part of an industry that many companies consider family. If you are hired, you are going to be at the business more than one quarter of the day. You are the greatest resource of the business because with your skills, work experience and education, you are valuable. The employer knows that managing people correctly can take up priceless production time. Therefore, to keep controversy to a minimum, the lawyers have given employers an employee blueprint on how to effectively hire and fire you. Beware!

- They are going to give you a ***Job Description***. They are going to imply, but not tell you that the job description clarifies your role fully. They use the job description to avoid mystification about your role, define the essential functions of the position, and to have a leg to stand on legally if you sue them later.

- They are going to provide you with a document generally termed an "***Employment Offer" or "Offer of Employment"***. This letter is designed with more structure than the Golden Gate Bridge. Lawyers advise companies to give you this letter before you start the job. They want you to read the letter and sign it. Once you have signed the employment letter and returned it to the employer, you have officially signed a *legal contract*, which in most cases will be careful not to provide you with a property interest in the position. If the employer does not tell you that there is a probationary period in the letter, they may have negated an important key regarding your employment rights.

- The ***Probationary period*** can be used as a tool to summarily fire you at any time during the specified time of probation. A usual feature of a probationary period is that the employer may end your employment without affording you a due process procedure that may be afforded to non-probationary employees. Usually a probationary period is ninety days. In most companies, employee's legal status is at will. Simply put, "at will" employees may be terminated for any legal reason at the discretion of the employer. The employer may fire the employee for anything, or the employee may leave for any reason without giving notice to the employer.

However, to play it smart, they may simply fire you without cause saying that you did not pass the probationary period and unless they have violated your ***protected rights***, there is little you can do about an "at will" firing. Generally, a private sector employee, who is not carried by a union, is "at will" under the law. Therefore, without a written employment contract, or prevailing enforceable verbal contract, an employer may without breaking the laws per se, fire an employee, so long as they do not breach a protected class or break the law. ***Remember:*** it is always wise to do your research, using the resources provided herein, and challenge an employer who fires you for no reason.

- Judges are keenly aware of the "at will" laws. They know the law allows employers to fire innocent people sometimes. Again, for probation to be sensible, and adequate, it has to be agreed upon between yourself and the employer before you start the job.

- *References*. **Employment Defense** Lawyers and other employer advocates believe that there are an increasing number of people providing false employment details and fake references to promote their bid for the job. *TIP:* They are telling the employer to confirm your references and to talk directly to past employers or they will use professional screening services to track down the truth. *Advice:* Be honest. Even if you had a bad relationship with a past employer, call them. Ask them to give you a start, and end date, of your last job on company letterhead. Tell them it is against the law to tell a future employer things about you that are not true. That way when you fill out an application for a new job, you have tangible proof from the Department of Human Resources that your dates are accurate. No company wants to risk a potential defamation lawsuit. Instead, your former company will be more than willing to give you a start and end date reference. You cannot always rely on friends or false references.

Employment Defense Lawyers and other employer advocates are telling the employer to settle. If the employer has not done things right by you from the beginning, they dig themselves a hole. Let me be honest. There are unqualified people wearing big hats in companies that do not know how to be fair to employees. Unprofessional behavior and incompetence on the part of the employer can cost time and money regardless whether the company at issue is right or wrong.

Good and fair employment practices are vital to a serious business. Good employment practice can reduce cost. Therefore, you can help your company maintain being a great employer by assuring yourself of the following:

Follow the company rules

Know your legal employee/employment rights

Keep your own paper trail to match or better employer

Stay calm, resolve work issues, try not to get fired

- Call your lawyer to read employment agreements, contracts

Chapter 16

Unemployment Insurance

There are numerous reasons why one may have to apply for unemployment insurance. Few persons have the time to really explain the importance of unemployment insurance and I have learned that there are many individuals who pay into this system and don't understand how the insurance applies to them. We're so engaged in looking for a job and keeping a job, sometimes unemployment comes into view as an aside. Remember when we talked about the Employee Handbook? Your Handbook will mention unemployment and how to apply for it, but the important details of unemployment are often overlooked in such text. Please understand that there are varying reasons why an employee can end up unemployed and you must clarify what happened first to an Administrative Law Judge and later to your next job. People are let go or terminated of employment at will or against their will. Don't let being terminated ruin your next steps in employment and never voluntarily quit a job! At Will, means the employer maintains the right to get rid of you at any time for any reason, it does not have to have rhyme or reason except if one of your statutory rights have been violated within the course of your work and then the firing becomes another ball game. Call Unemployment in your state!

Chapter 17

Fired/Unemployment II

1. Fired at will means for no reason, which is stipulated prior to your signing the employment contract.

2. Attendance, "no call" or "no show" One did not show up for work and did not bother to cal.

3. Drug use means you either flunked the standard drug test or were caught using on the job.

4. Drinking on the job mean that you were caught drinking on the job.

5. Imcompetence is that work performance does not meet stated duties on a consistent basis. (Make sure you receive warnings) before this is fulfilled in terms of a firing.

6. Misconduct mean poor behavior on the job against rules and policy.

7. Lying on the job application, means you were caught not telling the truth and the company found out and has to let you go unless you can prove otherwise.

8. Fighting on the job means that you have engaged in an altercation on the job with either management or another employee.

9. Insubordination a compilation of events proving you're not able to or are not willing to perform job duties.

10. Job Closed down means employees have been given due notice that the company is closing.

11. End of assignment means the date for you to be on the job has expired for whatever reasons.

For whatever reasons you're applying for unemployment, fight hard. Even if you're fired, fight for your unemployment. The administrative law judge is trained to understand the nuances of employment and how an employee may in fact be wrongfully terminated. Remember that if you apply for unemployment insurance and lose, always, always file for the 21-day appeal. Many cases have been won the second time up to bat. At this point you have nothing to lose.

If you are being fired, make them do it the right way!

Never *voluntarily quit* your job and lose dollars due to you under unemployment insurance. If you simply do not want to be fired, *(and you have another job lined up,)* then quitting would be a practicable option. In any case, if you are going to stick it out make sure the following things are in play before your employment with your job is terminated.

1. Make sure your employer has given you a fair chance to improve and prove to you in writing that you knew your job was at risk before the termination ensued.

2. Make sure the employer did not breach your employment contract.

3. Make sure the employer did not act intentionally to breach your contract.

4. Make sure the employer follows all federal laws regarding your final paycheck. It is California law to give you the final check <u>immediately</u> upon dismissal. *(This rule may not apply to other states.)*

5. Ask for severance pay and or all benefits due to you including stock options.

1. Apply for unemployment insurance the next working day that you are let go regardless if you are fired. If you lose unemployment benefits, you may win back wages in the California Unemployment Insurance appeals process.

<u>KNOW WHAT CLAIM TO FILE</u>

- A regular California claim if you worked in California in a job covered by the unemployment insurance law even if you now reside outside California.

- A federal claim if your employment was in civilian work for the federal government or as a member of the Armed Forces (*benefit costs are paid from federal funds*).

- An interstate claim if earnings were in another state. If you worked in another state in the last 24 months, you may be able to file a claim. This includes the District of Columbia, Canada, Puerto Rico, and the Virgin Islands.

- A combined wage claim if you have earnings in more than one state in specified times. This type of claim could increase your Unemployment Insurance benefits. For base periods and more, call one of the numbers below.

This example applies to California. Simply look up the same information in the state you live in. Begin by asking officials what the correct form is to fill out for your state.

Unemployment Insurance Call Information:

English: 1-800-300-5616 Vietnamese:
  1-800-547-2058

Spanish: 1-800-326-8937 TTY (Non-Voice)
  1-800-815-9387

Cantonese 1-800-547-3506

Chapter 18

Worker's Compensation II

Employee Guide to Worker's Compensation

Note: *Always Reference Current Workers Compensation Law*

You were hurt on the job. You are not sure what workers compensation is. Here is what you should do:

FIRST: Know that workers compensation is the insurance that the law requires your employer to have to help you when you get hurt on the job, or if you get sick because of your job.

REPORT: As soon as you get hurt on the job, *(no matter how minor you think that the injury is)* tell your supervisor that you have been hurt. Don't worry about how big or small the injury is report it, and the doctor appointed to treat you will diagnose your injury appropriately. If you are hurt on the job and no one is around call 911. Make sure you tell the emergency staff that your injury is a job related injury.

What happens next?

- A. Next, your employer will give you a claim form.

- B. Make sure the form is called: The Workers Compensation (**DWC 1**)

C. When you get the form complete the "Employee" section (only)

D. Give your completed (DWC1) form to your employer.

E. Keep a copy of this form until you get the signed and dated copy from your employer.

F. Make sure your injury is recorded on the 301 Form for your individual injury and make sure the manager updates all the appropriate logs.

G. Know: The Division of Workers Compensation #1-800-736-7401

What are my rights?

A. One day after you file a claim form, the law requires the employer to authorize medical treatment as required and limited by the law, until the claim is accepted or rejected.

B. You have a limit of $10,000.00 total.

C. If your claim is rejected, get a workers compensation attorney immediately!

How long do I have to file a claim?

A. You should tell your employer within 30 days of the date of injury.

B.   REMEMBER: you should always act quickly so as not to risk losing your benefits because you waited too long to report your injury.

If you are injured on the job, chances are you are going to be confused by the complicated process of Workers Compensation law. You are going to want to know what the process is. Even if your injury was a total acccident, chances are after you get hurt on the job your relationship at work will change. One way or another it will not be the same. Workers who are hurt are sometimes confused by the procedures.

Be sure: That you have a case and pursue your benefits fully. Look in the yellow pages for a Workers Compensation attorney. Familiarize your-self with each detail of what your case entails:

Temporary Disability

TD is paid at a weekly rate during the time the doctor says that the injured worker is unable to work because of the injury. TD is paid at the rate of two-thirds (66%) of the injured employees gross earnings up to the maximum that is set by law. The maximum rate for Temporary Disability is presently paid at the rate of $490.00 a week, *(see chart on the next page for additional rates)* for injuries that have occurred on or after January 01, 1996. Wait for first check: two-weeks.

Permanent Disability

For workers left with any residual disability they may be entitled to receive a *permanent disability award*. These monies are not payable until the medical condition becomes permanent and stationary, which means the physcian has signed off on the condition as having been leveled off and will stay substantially the same in the future. Remember: If the doctor says there has been a total recovery, there would be no permanent disability award.

> **Note:** *When dealing with Workers Compensation issues and or injuries, be smart. What may not hurt today, may sear tomorrow. If injured on the job, always negotiate for future medical awards for your injury where it is warranted.*

Medical Consultation

When the doctor ends your treatment and says that your medical condition may be permanent and stationary or that you can go back to work, get examined by a Qualified Medical Examiner. If you are not represented by an attorney, the insurance Company will send you the injured party, a list of doctors, (QME) to choose from. If you, the injured worker have a lawyer, your lawyer will choose the QME or make an agreement with the insurance Company to utilize QME.

Settlement of the Case

When all the medical reports are submitted with a detail narrative including professional opinions by all of your treating doctors, you may be ready to settle your case. The report will be rated and a percentage of disability will be assigned to the doctors opinions in accordance with the rating guidelines of the State of California. The rating percentage is then converted into a monetary settlement amount and all ratings and preset rating guidelines are arranged in accordance with a schedule.

> **Note:** *If you have been without an attorney before; now is the time to hire one. You will receive more of the benefits you deserve if you have an experienced lawyer to negotiate your case for you. Consult the State of California Bar Association or your yellow pages for a Workers Compensation Attorney.*

Rehabilitation

If you are not able to return to the job you had when you got injured; you may be eligible for rehabilitation. While you are pursuing rehabilitation training you will continue to receive either temporary disability benefits or a rehabilitation maintenance allowance.

Workers' Compensation Appeals Board

The Workers' Compensation Appeals Board is the state court for all industrial injuries involving your employer. The proceedings are administrative and there are not juries. Contact a office in your city for more information regarding your rights in Civil Court.

Important Points to Remember

If you are hurt on the job, no matter how minor it is, report it immediately, and demand, to see a doctor right away. An injury or illness that takes place due to your job is a workers' compensation injury or illness. If somebody tells you, "well, you picked up that box the wrong way! Had you picked it up right, you would not have gotten hurt." Say thank you to that person, then march right over to the telephone, call the HR person, tell them that you were hurt, and tell them to please send you all forms from BC to present for your injury. If there are witnesses that saw you get hurt never, feel embarrassed to write that person's name down or ask them to sign a declaration, and look up at the clock and right down the time you were hurt.

If they don't testify today because of fear, or out of losing their job; believe me, they will have to talk when you subpoena them later to come to the Worker's Compensation Appeals Board for adjudication of your claim. Honest employers recognize injuries, and they process such matters accordingly. But, remember:

"If you get hurt on the job, no matter how minor, tell somebody immediately."

Workers Compensation Attorneys are very busy. Your case is important to them. Therefore, please be considerate and keep in mind before calling about your case incessantly, see if you can handle some questions yourself first.

Carol Denise Mitchell

Listen to your attorney!

- I may not always be readily available

- You are not my only client

- I am at the board, a hearing or a conference OR adjudicating another case

- Your case is complicated to you; but, not to me

- You can call the insurance company yourself about your check

- You can call the insurance company yourself to change a doctor's appointment

- Call doctors (directly) to change appointment dates/times

- Do not sign anything without my advice

    California Experts to Contact:

    Nationwide Worker's Compensation

    Information Assistant Officers

California Division of Workers Compensation

Nationwide 1-800-421-3535

Chapter 19

EEOC

The Public's Overview of Federal Sector EEO Complaint Process

If you are a federal employee or job applicant, the law protects you from discrimination because of your race, color, religion, sex (including gender identity, sexual orientation, and pregnancy), national origin, age (40 or older), disability or genetic information. The law also protects you from retaliation if you oppose employment discrimination, file a complaint of discrimination, or participate in the EEO complaint process (even if the complaint is not yours.)

There are also federal laws and regulations and Executive Orders (which are not enforced by EEOC) that prohibit discrimination on bases such as sexual orientation, marital status, parental status, or political affiliation.

If you are a federal employee or job applicant and you believe that a federal agency has discriminated against you, you have a right to file a complaint. Each agency is required to post information about how to contact the agency's EEO Office. You can contact an EEO Counselor by calling the office responsible for the agency's EEO complaints program.

Carol Denise Mitchell

EEO Counselor

The first step is to contact an EEO Counselor at the agency where you work or where you applied for a job. Generally, you must contact the EEO Counselor within 45 days from the day the discrimination occurred.

In most cases the EEO Counselor will give you the choice of participating either in EEO counseling or in an alternative dispute resolution (ADR) program, such as a mediation program.

If you do not settle the dispute during counseling or through ADR, you can file a formal discrimination complaint against the agency with the agency's EEO Office. You must file within 15 days from the day you receive notice from your EEO Counselor about how to file.

Filing A Formal Complaint

Once you have filed a formal complaint, the agency will review the complaint and decide whether the case should be dismissed for a procedural reason (for example, your claim was filed too late).

If the agency doesn't dismiss the complaint, it will investigate. The agency has 180 days from the day you filed your complaint to finish the investigation.

When the investigation is finished, the agency will issue a notice giving you two choices: either request a hearing before an EEOC Administrative Judge or ask the agency to issue a decision as to whether the discrimination occurred.

Agency Issues A Decision (Final Action)

If you ask the agency to issue a decision and no discrimination is found, or if you disagree with some part of the decision, you can appeal the decision to EEOC or challenge it in federal district court.

Requesting A Hearing

If you want to ask for a hearing, you must make your request in writing or via the EEOC Public Portal located at https://publicportal.eeoc.gov/ where you can also upload hearing requests, and manage your personal and representative information within 30 days from the day you receive the notice from the agency about your hearing rights. If you request a hearing, an EEOC Administrative Judge will conduct the hearing, make a decision, and order relief if discrimination is found.

Once the agency receives the Administrative Judge's decision, the agency will issue what is called a final order which will tell you whether the agency agrees with the Administrative Judge and if it will grant any relief the judge ordered. The agency will have 40 days to issue the final order. It will also contain information about your right to appeal to EEOC, your right to file a civil action in federal district court, and the deadline for filing both an appeal and a civil action.

Carol Denise Mitchell

Filing an Appeal of The Agency's Final Order

You have the right to appeal an agency's final order (including a final order dismissing your complaint) to EEOC Office of Federal Operations. You must file your appeal no later than 30 days after you receive the final order. You may file your appeal using the EEOC's Public Portal located at https://publicportal.eeoc.gov/ where you can also upload selected documents and manage your personal and representative information.

EEOC appellate attorneys will review the entire file, including the agency's investigation, the decision of the Administrative Judge, the transcript of what was said at the hearing (if there was a hearing), and any appeal statements.

If the agency disagrees with any part of the Administrative Judge's decision, it must appeal to EEOC.

Request for Reconsideration of The Appeal Decision

If you do not agree with the EEOC's decision on your appeal, you can ask for a reconsideration of that decision. A request for reconsideration is only granted if you can show that the decision is based on a mistake about the facts of the case or the law applied to the facts. You must ask for reconsideration no later than 30 days after you receive our decision on your appeal.

Once EEOC has issued a decision on the appeal, the agency also has the right to ask EEOC to reconsider that decision.

Once we have decided on your request for reconsideration, the decision is final.

Right to Sue -Filing A Lawsuit

You must go through the administrative complaint process before you can file a lawsuit and remember what I told you about exhausting all in-house opportunities with your employer before pursuing a case with the EEOC. Otherwise, no matter how great your case is, you may lose for not following the Employee Handbook to the "T".

There are several different points during the process; however, when you will have the opportunity to quit the process and file a lawsuit in court, including:

After 180 days have passed from the day you filed your complaint, if the agency has not issued a decision and no appeal has been filed

Within 90 days from the day you receive the agency's decision on your complaint, so long as no appeal has been filed

After the 180 days from the day you filed your appeal if the EEOC has not issued a decision, or

Within 90 days from the day you receive the EEOC's decision on your appeal.

Carol Denise Mitchell

Employee's Resources Sheet

National Employment Law Firm: (877) 783-4729

National Worker's Compensation and Disability Conference: (800) 727-1227

United States Department of Labor - 1-866-487-2635

Equal Employment Opportunity Commission - (800) 669-4000

<u>Civil Rights Center (CRC)</u>

1-202-693-6500

Hours: Monday to Friday, 8:00 a.m. to 5:00 p.m. EST

<u>Office of Labor-Management Standards (OLMS)</u>

1-202-693-0123

Hours: Monday to Friday, 8:00 a.m. to 5:00 p.m. EST

<u>Office of Workers' Compensation Programs (OWCP)</u>

1-202-693-0036

Hours: Monday to Friday, 8:30 a.m. to 4:45 p.m. EST

<u>Wage and Hour Division (WHD)</u>

1-866-4-US-WAGE (1-866-487-9243)

Hours: Monday to Friday, 8 a.m. to 8 p.m. EST

Employee required benefits on the job

What Are Required Employee Benefits?

Social Security and Medicare Benefits. Every employer, regardless of size, is subject to the required employee benefit of matching their employees' social security and Medicare contributions. ...

1. Unemployment Insurance. ...
2. Worker's Compensation. ...
3. Disability Insurance. ...
4. Family Medical Leave Benefits. ...
5. Health Insurance.

Carol Denise Mitchell

"Final Message to Readers"

American workers have effectively served this Country well for centuries. Consequently, we are easily led by conscience to hurry into another job before claiming that which is rightfully ours from the old Company that let us go. If a Company feels puissant enough to let you go easily; you must find your endurance to fight them and guard your good name. Your work record is life-long. So, turn around, take care of your business, and preserve your work record before running into another job.

Never blame yourself for being methodically and uniformly fired. Today's workforce is subjective and intractable enough for anyone to be fired or replaced at a moment's notice. I know that because it has happened to me before. As an aging working professional, I have managed three large companies. In those jobs, my duties required me to work with employees from a variety of beautiful national cultures. The most difficult thing I ever had to do on a job was let someone go, but I was always proud to see workers stand up to large companies and to me, to defend their employment rights.

Caught up in the capitalistic goals of businesses and mergers in the free world, commerce competitiveness here and abroad bred an aggressive industry with exceptional opportunities for vast and expansive growth. However, I have watched firsthand the use for older workers diminish significantly in this Country to a point we were woefully forced out of old industry, as new and younger workers came into our jobs to handle new core concepts inside an ever-changing, complicated technological boom in the American workplace. The augmentation of computers and automation eliminated many jobs in short notice and corporations got avaricious enough to ask for a cut of some workers hard earned benefits and to my dismay some courts granted such request. Consequently, as a growing number of American workers find themselves fired or laid off and replaced by youngsters, computers and automation, this incalculable informational handbook will make it much easier for all workers to defend their rights, and hard-earned benefits in the American workplace.

When you are being fired, the process is carried out in an intricate, and well-organized routine that is predicated usually on rigid boardroom demands or numbers that were crunched by people who did not visually see your great contributions to their business or industry. Corporate decisions generally are final and leave no room for job resumption for the exiting employee. Firing such workers got depressing enough for me not to want to fire people anymore. I saw fewer exiting employees who challenged these corporate decisions. I got worried. I watched helpless as many of them left behind valuable employment earnings and assets to rush responsibly and sometimes un-responsibly into another job.

Those words being said, there are still many great companies in operation that believes in their employees, and you may just be working for one of them. Constantly observe the changes in your company today and on a regular basis.

It is key for you to understand your ***"Employment Offer Letter."*** Be prepared for transition by viewing and acknowledging the real possibilities of change.

I wrote this book for you, America's greatest asset! If you did not get what you deserved in your last job, use the knowledge that you gain from this handbook to bargain next time for a better working contract. Ask an employment law attorney to review your new or old employment contract and help you negotiate for benefits that you deserve. You are a gem. Your strong work experience is priceless, and you should get paid for your educational value and all of your work life experiences. I encourage you to protect yourself. Keep this employment informational guide at your easy dispense and utilize this manual to find out about important and meaningful aspects of how to preserve your longevity in today's American workforce and much more. I dedicate this book to America's working-class employees. I hope that I have been able to help you understand your work rights better. May all that this book contains assist you and yours for many years to come. Good Luck!

incalculable informational handbook will make it much easier for all workers to defend their rights, and hard-earned benefits in the American workplace.

When you are being fired, the process is carried out in an intricate, and well-organized routine that is predicated usually on rigid boardroom demands or numbers that were crunched by people who did not visually see your great contributions to their business or industry. Corporate decisions generally are final and leave no room for job resumption for the exiting employee. Firing such workers got depressing enough for me not to want to fire people anymore. I saw fewer exiting employees who challenged these corporate decisions. I got worried. I watched helpless as many of them left behind valuable employment earnings and assets to rush responsibly and sometimes un-responsibly into another job.

Those words being said, there are still many great companies in operation that believes in their employees, and you may just be working for one of them. Constantly observe the changes in your company today and on a regular basis.

It is key for you to understand your *"Employment Offer Letter."* Be prepared for transition by viewing and acknowledging the real possibilities of change.

I wrote this book for you, America's greatest asset! If you did not get what you deserved in your last job, use the knowledge that you gain from this handbook to bargain next time for a better working contract. Ask an employment law attorney to review your new or old employment contract and help you negotiate for benefits that you deserve. You are a gem. Your strong work experience is priceless, and you should get paid for your educational value and all of your work life experiences. I encourage you to protect yourself. Keep this employment informational guide at your easy dispense and utilize this manual to find out about important and meaningful aspects of how to preserve your longevity in today's American workforce and much more. I dedicate this book to America's working-class employees. I hope that I have been able to help you understand your work rights better. May all that this book contains assist you and yours for many years to come. Good Luck!

incalculable informational handbook will make it much easier for all workers to defend their rights, and hard-earned benefits in the American workplace.

When you are being fired, the process is carried out in an intricate, and well-organized routine that is predicated usually on rigid boardroom demands or numbers that were crunched by people who did not visually see your great contributions to their business or industry. Corporate decisions generally are final and leave no room for job resumption for the exiting employee. Firing such workers got depressing enough for me not to want to fire people anymore. I saw fewer exiting employees who challenged these corporate decisions. I got worried. I watched helpless as many of them left behind valuable employment earnings and assets to rush responsibly and sometimes un-responsibly into another job.

Those words being said, there are still many great companies in operation that believes in their employees, and you may just be working for one of them. Constantly observe the changes in your company today and on a regular basis.

It is key for you to understand your *"Employment Offer Letter."* Be prepared for transition by viewing and acknowledging the real possibilities of change.

I wrote this book for you, America's greatest asset! If you did not get what you deserved in your last job, use the knowledge that you gain from this handbook to bargain next time for a better working contract. Ask an employment law attorney to review your new or old employment contract and help you negotiate for benefits that you deserve. You are a gem. Your strong work experience is priceless, and you should get paid for your educational value and all of your work life experiences. I encourage you to protect yourself. Keep this employment informational guide at your easy dispense and utilize this manual to find out about important and meaningful aspects of how to preserve your longevity in today's American workforce and much more. I dedicate this book to America's working-class employees. I hope that I have been able to help you understand your work rights better. May all that this book contains assist you and yours for many years to come. Good Luck! Stay tuned for the "Employee's Only Checklist Smart Sheet!" Use this form to keep track of work projects, Copy and file, in case you need to reference the sheet later.

EMPLOYMENT SMART FACT SHEET

YOUR NAME

YOUR JOB TITLE

YOUR START DATE

DAILY NOTES SHEET/OTHER PROJECTS

1
2
3
4
5
6
7
8
9
10

QUICK REFERENCE GUIDE	
NAME	NUMBER
NAME	NUMBER
NAME	NUMBER
NAME	NUMBER
NAME	NUMBER

Use this sheet to writer down important work contacts. Copy this sheet as many times as you like. Neatly store for quick reference.

Chapter 20

FREE Mobile Apps for Job Search

1. Indeed, Job search

Desktop Job Boards for uploading your resume to apply really easy. Search based. Will require you to fill out job search information that may include cover letters, portfolios and samples. So, get going on that handy device.

2. You can get the CareerBuilder download on iOS on you Android

Comprehensive tool for all facets of the job search, including making great resumes and right there you can use the resume to apply for jobs. You'll get alerts that will let you know when your resume was viewed and what company looked at it. Job searching is simple and easy with the artificial intelligence and augmented reality powered app. Humair Gauri, CareerBuilder's Chief Product Officer, says, "We can tell you which jobs are in your immediate vicinity or any designated distance and provide an augmented reality view of job openings – and what they pay — as you walk by businesses. Our local targeting provides a map view and list view of jobs and serves up an entirely different experience for job seekers." In addition, the app sends notifications on new job openings based on the job seekers' preferences and show higher paying jobs with information on acquiring the skills needed to get to the next level. Users can use the tools to start planning for the next stage of their career.

3. Glassdoor

Very similar to its much-heralded desktop experience, Glassdoor allows mobile users to both access thousands of up-to-date job listings while getting first-hand knowledge of companies from current and former employees. The app is segmented into different categories – jobs, companies, salaries and interviews – and can feel a little overwhelming to navigate. Much like the Glassdoor desktop experience, the company reviews and employee insights are the attraction here. Filling out full applications via your mobile device?

4. Snagajob

The premiere mobile job app for hourly employees, Snagajob understands that the non-salary workforce needs to move fast. After importing your social profile from Facebook or Google and filling in personal details, browse hourly positions in your area and click to apply. Filter positions by Schedule (part-time, seasonal, summer jobs) and Type of Job (automotive, construction, food & restaurant) and Distance. The app also features a handy map function to show you the company's location. Drawbacks? While Snagajob has many jobs that need just a single click to apply, some require a longer application process, and the lack of skilled, salaried positions can feel limiting.

5. Good.Co

The job search is as much about self-discovery as it is job discovery, and Good.Co is a useful reminder of that fact. The app users find companies and careers that will benefit their overall wellbeing, not just their bank account. Through personality quizzes like What Are Your Unique Strengths? and How Do You Come Across to Others, Good.Co unlocks increasingly nuanced insights about yourself and offers you companies and jobs that might match your personality and working style. You cannot apply to these jobs within the app, but instead are redirected back to major job boards for that part of the process.

6. Simply Hired

Another job aggregator Simply Hired has a continuously improving mobile app interface. Recently, they added features that allow job seekers to sort their job searches by date and relevance, in an attempt to relieve the crushing weight of endless job scrolling. Your homepage includes your recent searches and it is easy to save and share jobs. Like other search apps, though, Simply Hired seems to have one foot in mobile and the other on desktop. For example, some jobs allow one-touch mobile applications, while others require you to upload a resume and even a cover letter.

Tips for Using Job Search Apps

How can you get the most out of the apps you're using to streamline your job search? These tips will help you search and apply for jobs and connect with hiring managers, with just a few taps on your phone or tablet.

Distill your resume to fit on a smartphone screen. Forget your traditional one-page CV. Mobile job apps require an even more succinct display of your skills and experience. If formulated correctly, less can be more. Be certain to prioritize your most marketable credentials to capture the hiring manager's attention. Forcing yourself to distill your background in this way will help you have a better understanding of your professional self and eventually help you better market yourself in networking and interview situations.

Know the keywords. The best job apps use smart algorithms to match relevant candidates with open jobs and vice-versa. These algorithms rely on keywords that illustrate certain experiences and skills, those that candidates may possess, and job listings may include as requirements for a position. If you're a salesperson with expertise in channel sales, for example, ensure you've listed that under your skills. Clarity is vital. Save the nuance for after you connect with a hiring manager.

Polish your profile. A great photo, a compelling headline, and a clear outline of skills and experience can help separate you from the crowd and inject some much-needed personality into your professional profile. Stand out but try to limit confusing or cute language and images.

Tips:

Be professional. Even if you're using a job app on your phone, you still must abide by the rules of professionalism when corresponding with employers. Sure, the dialogue and environment feel refreshingly casual and stress-free, but you must remain vigilant about accuracy, proper grammar, attention to detail, and professional etiquette. You might be tapping to apply to jobs and "texting" with hiring managers, but always remember that this isn't social media - our professional future is at stake!

ABOUT THE AUTHOR

2011 award-winning writer Carol Denise Mitchell began writing as a youngster when she learned her father was illiterate and could not read. The author was born on May 12, 1955, in Los Angeles, California, and is the sixth of sixteen children. She is the daughter of Zebbie Thomas Charles, Sr., and Tasceaie Carise Charles. Mitchell was reared in Los Angeles, during the noteworthy era of the Civil Rights Movement. During an interview with the Oakland, Tribune, she recalled living in an Urban setting in Watts, California, during an era in American history that became a motivating influence behind her writing career, when three-days of rioting in August 1965 changed her life.

"I remember the Watts Riot, I was encouraged by my mother that change, degradation, and Urban ruin, would be a motivating factor for us all to grow." After this time in history, Mitchell began steadily leaving her imprint on fighting illiteracy. Hence, Mitchell wrote many notable novels, including "Your Rights, What Employers do not want you to know," getting critical acclaim by lawyers and unions in the work industry. Next, she chronicled her early life in an award-winning novel, What Happened to Suzy, winning praise for its' message of healing and hope.

In Oakland, California Mitchell worked alongside slain newspaper Editor, Chauncey Bailey as a news reporter for [Soul Beat]. She was highlighted in The Oakland Post Newspaper, for her groundbreaking work as a writer. Mitchell is an expert niche writer for E-zine Articles. Mitchell's latest projects are represented on her author's page. Her books have garnered buyers in Australia, The United Kingdom, Italy and around the world. Mitchell currently resides in Phoenix, Arizona

www.ingramcontent.com/pod-product-compliance
Lightning Source LLC
Chambersburg PA
CBHW022006170526
45157CB00003B/1166